ISBN 978-1-331-97003-3
PIBN 10262035

FB &c Ltd, Dalton House, 60 Windsor Avenue, London, SW19 2RR.
Company number 08720141. Registered in England and Wales.

For support please visit www.forgottenbooks.com

APPLIED MOTION STUDY

A COLLECTION OF PAPERS
ON
THE EFFICIENT METHOD TO
INDUSTRIAL PREPAREDNESS

BY

FRANK B. GILBRETH
Consulting Management Engineer
Member Franklin Institute; American Society of Mechanical Engineers; Society for the Promotion of Engineering Education

AND

L. M. GILBRETH, Ph.D.

New York
STURGIS & WALTON
COMPANY
1917

Set up and electrotyped. Published, September, 1917.

PREFACE

This book aims —

1. To describe Motion Study as applied to various fields of activity.
2. To outline the principles and practice of Motion Study in such a way as to make possible its application in any and all kinds of work.

Motion Study is a means to permanent and practical waste elimination,— hence a prerequisite to efficient preparedness that shall be adequate, constructive and cumulative.

FOREWORD

This book aims to present in outline

1. The field where motion study has been and can be applied.
2. The methods by which it is applied.
3. The effects of the application.

It shows the results of actual practice in waste elimination. It enumerates past savings, and points out present and future possible savings.

It is offered as a contribution to the solution of the great national problem of "Preparedness."

INTRODUCTION

Blessed is the man who makes two blades of grass grow where only one grew before. More blessed is he who multiplies the harvests of toil not merely two-fold, but three-fold or more-fold, for he virtually lengthens life when he adds to its fruitage. Such a man is Frank B. Gilbreth who tells in this book just how he wrought this wonder. For years he has closely watched workers at tasks of all kinds; he has discovered how much they lose by moving unprofitably hither and thither, by neglecting to take the shortest and easiest paths. In the ancient trade of bricklaying he has increased the output almost four-fold by doing only what must be done, and using a few simple devices of his own invention. In this volume Mr. Gilbreth describes and pictures the simple photographic process which enables one to record in detail the motions of a handicraft, or a manufacture, so as to bring them by criticism and experiment to their utmost economy of energy and time. When once the best practice is reached in any particular field of work

Gilbreth motion-pictures make it easy to repeat that practice anywhere and at any time.

This most fertile means of record and of teaching enters the world of industry at an opportune moment. War to-day is destroying wealth at a rate beyond computation. National debts are mounting billion upon billion, entailing burdens of taxation such as mankind never faced before. Mr. Gilbreth meets this dire emergency with a readily applied method of increasing the results of toil, of reducing all waste of human exertion to its minimum. Not the least telling branch of his activity is in extending aid and comfort to maimed soldiers. He opens a door of hope, because a door of usefulness, to the thousands of brave men who have lost their limbs, their sight, or their hearing, on fields of battle.

His pages teem with suggestive facts: take, for example, his discovery that the best way to perform a task unites the methods of several dexterous and original operators. Again we are shown that wisdom rests not even with the most gifted man, but appears only when men of the rarest ability join hands. Another point: our author has found that learners should strive first for Quickness; when speed is acquired they can best pass to good quality in their work. The levy paid for Dawdling is plainly beyond all estimate. A third point: Mr. Gilbreth argues that to repeat a task should not mean monotony. Let a task be fully studied, let all its possibilities be brought into view, and the operator will be too keenly interested to complain of "monotony."

This is a book written from the heart as well as from the brain. Its good will is as evident as its good sense. Frank B. Gilbreth is a versatile Engineer, an untiring observer, an ingenious inventor, an economist to the tips of his fingers: first and chiefly he is a man. To his wife, co-author with him, this book owes much. Every page has taken form with the aid and counsel of Mrs. Gilbreth, whose "Psychology of Management" is a golden gift to industrial philosophy. And thus, by viewing their facts from two distinct angles we learn how vital phases of industrial economy present themselves to a man and to a woman who are among the acutest investigators of our time.

GEORGE ILES.

New York, June 14, 1917.

TABLE OF CONTENTS

CHAPTER III

CHAPTER IV

CHAPTER V

CHRONOCYCLEGRAPH MOTION DEVICES FOR MEASURING ACHIEVEMENT 73–96

CHAPTER VI

PAGE

MOTION MODELS: THEIR USE IN THE TRANSFERENCE OF EXPERIENCE AND THE PRESENTATION OF COMPARATIVE RESULTS IN EDUCATIONAL METHODS 97–130

CHAPTER VII

MOTION STUDY FOR THE CRIPPLED SOLDIER 131–157

CHAPTER VIII

CHAPTER IX

CHAPTER X PAGE

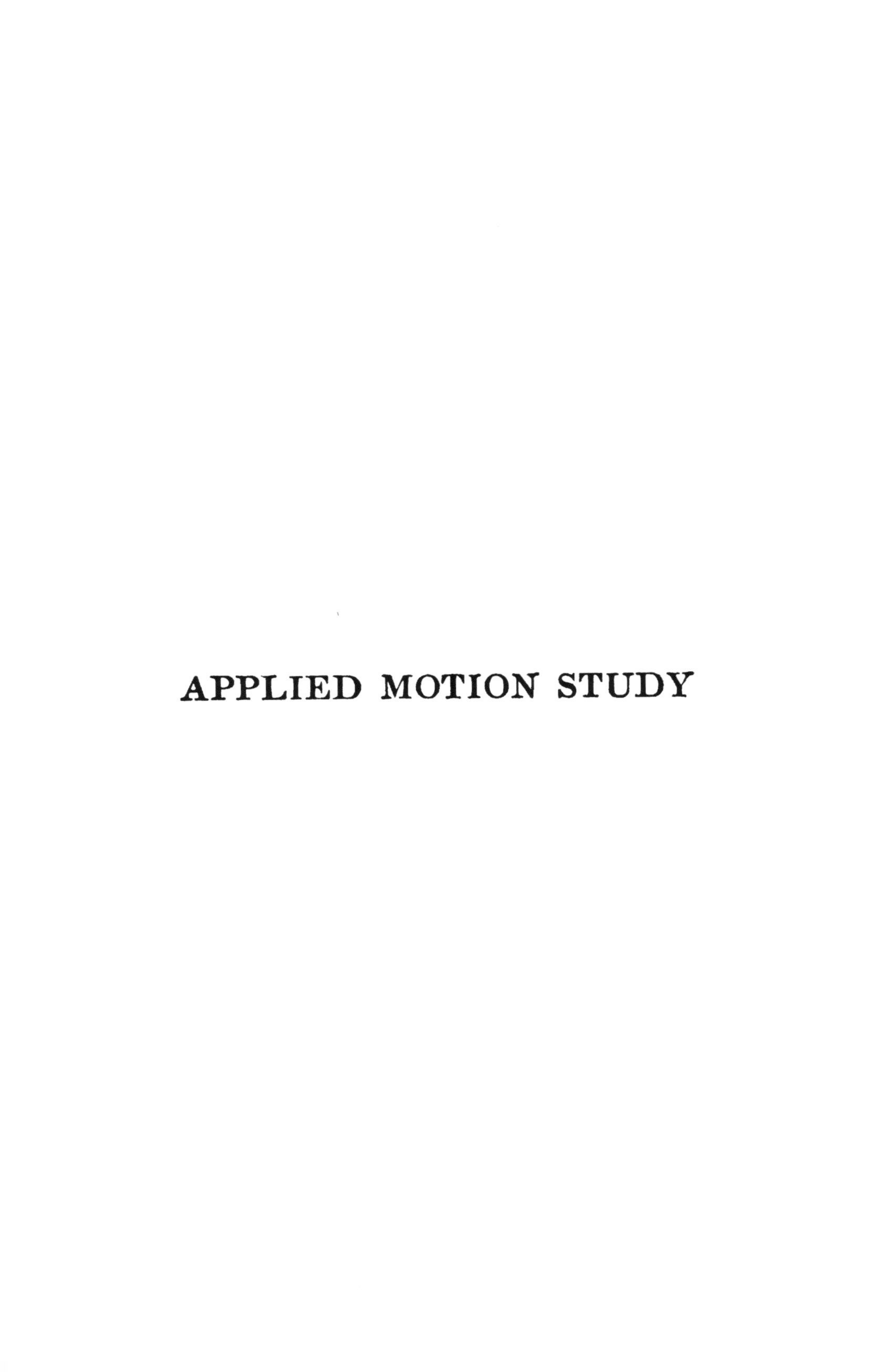

APPLIED MOTION STUDY

APPLIED MOTION STUDY

WHAT SCIENTIFIC MANAGEMENT MEANS TO AMERICA'S INDUSTRIAL POSITION[1]

There is some confusion to-day as to the meaning of scientific management. This concerns itself with the nature of such management itself, with the scope or field to which such management applies, and with the aims that it desires to attain. Scientific management is simply management that is based upon actual measurement. Its skilful application is an art that must be acquired, but its fundamental principles have the exactness of scientific laws which are open to study by every one. We have here nothing hidden or occult or secret, like the working practices of an old-time craft; we have here a science that is the result of accurately recorded, exact investigation. Its results are formulated, or are being

[1] Reprinted from "The Annals" of the American Academy of Political and Social Science, Publication No. 935.

formulated, into such shape that they may be utilised by all who have the desire to study them and the concentration to master them. The leaders in the field are, as rapidly as possible, publishing these results, that progress may take place from the stage of highest present achievement, and that no time or effort may be wasted in remaking investigations whose results are already known and accurately recorded. The scope of this management, which may truly be called scientific, is unlimited. It applies to all fields of activity, mental and physical. Its laws are universal, and, to be of use in any particular field, require only to be translated into the vocabulary of the trained and progressive workers in that field.

The greatest misunderstandings occur as to the aims of scientific management. Its fundamental aim is the elimination of waste, the attainment of worth-while desired results with the least necessary amount of time and effort. Scientific management may, and often does, result in expansion, but its primary aim is conservation and savings, making an adequate use of every ounce of energy of any type that is expended.

Scientific management, then, in attacking any problem has in mind the question — How may what is here available be best used? It considers the problem, in every case, according to the scientific method; that is, by dividing it into its elements and submitting each one of these to detailed study. Every problem presents two elements: the human element, and the materials element. By the materials element we mean the type of material used, the quality of material used, the quantity of material used, the manner in which the material is used, with conclusions as to why the material is chosen and handled as it is. In other words, we would apply to the material the familiar questions, what, how much, how, when, where, and why. These same questions are applied to the human element; that is to say, to all members of the organisation.

Having in mind now the principles and practice of scientific management, we can consider its relation to the industrial position of any country. Industrial growth, like all other growth, consists of progress and maintenance; that is, of advances over and beyond present achievement and of making adequate provision for holding any advantage that one may gain. It is generally realised that maintenance contains always the thought of conservation, that it is impossible to hold any advantage without making careful provision for using one's resources in the best possible manner. It is not so generally realised that progress also implies constantly this same conservation. The reason for this is the result of a confusion between saving, or conserving, and hoarding. True conservation contains no thought of miserliness or niggardliness. It is based upon a broad outlook on life and upon the needs of the situation, upon a willingness to pay the full, just price for what is wanted, but an unwillingness to pay any more than is necessary. Progress differs from lack of progress, fundamentally, not because the progressive man is willing to pay more than the unprogressive man will, but because the progressive man has a broader outlook and a keener insight, hence, a more adequate knowledge of where and when it is necessary to pay. The unprogressive man or nation suffers from a limited outlook that makes it practically impossible to make a just estimate as to what is worth while.

When we compare the various countries of the

world, and try to estimate their relative industrial positions, we find a strong relationship between conservation in its highest sense and industrial supremacy. Again, as we turn to history, we find this same relationship constantly manifesting itself; that is, progress depending upon an ability to see what is worth-while, and a willingness to pay for that and that only, and stability or maintenance depending upon an efficient handling of available resources.

As we review history, and observe present conditions, we see that the differences between various countries are becoming less and less, as time goes on. Transportation, with its numerous by-products that affect both the material and the human element, is increasing the likeness between different countries at an astounding rate. This means that industrial supremacy will depend more and more upon the handling of available resources and less and less upon distinctive features in these resources themselves. The calamitous war, which is now apparently offering such a serious check to industrial progress, is contributing toward ultimately making working conditions more similar, in that many countries are being thrown upon their own resources for both materials and men, and are being forced to make discoveries that will more nearly equalise these resources.

Another outcome of this war, that should prove of advantage to the world, is the emphasis that is being laid upon the causes of industrial position and industrial supremacy and the resulting study that is being made as to the reasons for such supremacy. Such a study should be particularly profitable here in America. This country has always "conceded" her important industrial position. She has realised thoroughly her enormous natural resources and also her wonderful human resources in that she is "the melting pot of the nations." It is only within the lifetime of those still young among us that we have come to realise the necessity of conserving our natural resources. It has not yet reached the attention of many among us that our human resources are as worthy, in fact, infinitely more worthy, of being conserved.

It is self-evident, then, that to attain and maintain an industrial position of which she may be proud, America must conserve both her natural and her human resources. If she hopes for industrial supremacy, she must set about this conservation with energy, and must pursue it unremittently.

The writers have a thorough knowledge of European industrial conditions, through having done business simultaneously in this country and abroad for many years, through frequent trips abroad before the war, through having crossed the boundaries of many of the warring countries many times since the outbreak of the war, and through having observed carefully industrial conditions and methods. Their opinion, which is that of all who have made intensive studies of these conditions, is that America is far behind European countries in conservation of the materials element, both natural and manufactured resources. This statement needs no proof in this place. The fact it contains is universally accepted by serious thinkers and investigators. It is equally true that up to recent times European countries have done comparatively little toward conserving the human element.

The hope of this country lies, then, in equalling or surpassing foreign conservation of material and in maintaining or progressing beyond our present conservation of the human element. The material problem is being attacked along different lines in a more or less systematic manner. We all appreciate the benefits of scientific or intensive farming, until now our native farmers, working under the direction of and with the co-operation of the Department of Agriculture, get results that equal those of European farmers, in their native lands, or here in ours. The importance of laboratory analysis of materials and the help that applied science can render and is more and more rendering to the industries are also being recognised. Agricultural experience has taught the valuable lesson that it is possible to get great output, yet, at the same time, leave the producing force unimpaired, by a proper expenditure of money and brains. Experience with applied science has taught that by-products, as well as products, must be considered, and that the exact methods of science often bring results that are beyond those looked for or hoped for. It has been common practice to consider a transaction satisfactory, or better, if it fulfilled one's expectations, to lay emphasis upon the result rather than to standardise the means or method. Laboratory practice has taught that while the immediate results are important, the standardisation of the method is more important, since the unexpected ultimate results, sometimes called by-products, are often by far the most valuable outcome of the work. Certain industries in this country have gone far toward applying scientific methods to the material element, but no one of us need go outside his own experience to be able to mention other industries that as yet have no conception of what such work means.

Much has been done not only in the analysis of materials, but also with the handling of materials. America has cause to be proud of her machines and her tools. The chief criticism that we may make of present practice in this field is that of lack of standardisation. The reasons for this are many. One is business competition, though the feeling is gradually dying out that making one's product markedly different from that of all others is a strong selling advantage. Another is the strong feeling of independence and individuality that leads one to prefer a thing because it is different rather than because it is adequate to the purpose for which it is needed. A third is a lack of channels for direct and easy communication of ideas. This is being supplied both through organisations and publications. A fourth is the former lack of standardising bodies or bureaus, a lack which is also being supplied as the demand for such bodies increases.

Because of the highly specialised nature of much present-day work, few of us realise how widespread, almost universal, the lack of standardisation is. It is only necessary to turn, however, to such a field of activity as surgery, which engages the attention of some of the finest brains in the country, and which is apt to come, sooner or later in some way, into the field of experience of every one, to see a striking object lesson of lack of standardisation both of tools and of method.

It is the work of scientific management to insist on standardisation in all fields, and to base such standardisation upon accurate measurement. Scientific management is not remote, or different from other fields of activity. For example, in the handling of the materials element, it does not attempt to discard the methods of attack of intensive agriculture or of the laboratory of the applied scientists; on the contrary, it uses the results of workers in such fields as these to as great an extent as possible.

There is a widespread feeling that scientific management claims to be something new, with methods that are different from those used by other conserving activities. This is not at all the case. It is the boast of scientific management that it gathers together the results and methods of all conserving activities, formulates these into a working practice, and broadens their field of application. In handling the materials element, then, scientific management analyses all successful existing practices in every line, and synthesises such elements as accurate measurement proves to be valuable into standards. These standards are maintained until suggested improvements have passed the same rigid examination, and are in such form that they may be incorporated into new standards.

Turning now to the field of the human element — by far the more important field — we find that, while there is much talk of work in that field to-day, comparatively little has actually been accomplished. There have, in all places and times, been more or less spasmodic and unsystematic attempts to conserve human energy, or to use it for the greatest benefit of all concerned; but there has not been steady and conspicuous progress in this work for several reasons; 1. Because the methods used were not accurately measured and were not standardised. This made it impossible for the individual conserver to accomplish much of lasting benefit. 2. Because of lack of co-operation between such conservers.

It is the task of scientific management to supply both these wants. Success in handling the human element, like success in handling the materials element, depends upon knowledge of the element itself and knowledge as to how it can best be handled. One great work of scientific management has been to show the world how little actual knowledge it has possessed of the human element as engaged in the work in the industries. Through motion study and fatigue study and the accompanying time study, we have come to know the capabilities of the worker, the demands of the work, the fatigue that the worker suffers at the work, and the amount and nature of the rest required to overcome the fatigue.

Those not actively interested in the industries can scarcely realise that the process of keeping the soil at its full producing capacity and of providing depleted energy is infinitely more standardised and more widely used than the process of providing that the human organism overcome fatigue and return to its normal working capacity in the shortest amount of time possible. Scientific provision for such recovery in the industries, before the days of scientific management, was unknown.

It is even more surprising that only the pioneers in the work realise the application of any necessity for the laboratory method in the study of the human element as it appears in the industries. When making accurate measurements, the number of variables involved must be reduced to as great a degree as possible. Only in the laboratory can this be successfully done. It is fortunate for scientific management that its initial introduction in the industries has been made by engineers rather than by men who are primarily laboratory scientists, for this reason: the engineer has been forced by his training to consider constantly immediate as well as ultimate results, and resent as well as future savings. Investigations of scientific management have, therefore, been made to pay from the start in money savings, as well as in savings of energy of all kinds. We note this in the results of motion study, fatigue study, and the accompanying time study.

As an example, take the laboratory investigations in motion study. These, where possible, are made by us in the laboratory, which is a room specially set apart in the plant for research purposes. Here the worker to be studied, with the necessary apparatus for doing the work and for measuring the motions, and the observer, investigate the operation under typical laboratory conditions. The product of this is data that are more nearly accurate than could be secured with the distractions and many variables of shop conditions. The by-product of this work, which is a typical by-product of engineer-scientists' work, is that the conditions of performing the operation in the laboratory become a practical working model of what the shop conditions must ultimately be. When the best method of doing the work with the existing apparatus has been determined in the laboratory, the working conditions, as well as the motions that make this result possible, are standardised, and the working conditions in the shop are changed, until they resemble the working conditions in the laboratory. In the same way, the length and periodicity of intervals to be allowed for overcoming fatigue, and the best devices for eliminating unnecessary fatigue and for overcoming necessary fatigue, are determined during the investigation, and are incorporated into shop practice.

The various measurements taken by scientific management and the guiding laws under which these are grouped determine not only the nature of the human element, but the methods by which it is to be handled. Motion study, fatigue study, the measures supplied by psychology,— these result in the working practice that fits the work to the worker, and produces more output with less effort, with its consequent greater pay for every ounce of effort expended.

Through scientific management, then, the individual conserver is enabled to progress constantly and to maintain each successful stage in the development. Scientific management can, also, and does, wherever permitted, provide for co-operation among conservers. It does this by:

1. Demonstrating the enormous waste resulting from needless repetition of the same investigation.
2. Providing standards which must be recognised as worthy of adoption, since they are the results of measurement.
3. Emphasising the importance of teaching and of the transference of skill, which depend upon co-operation.
4. Showing that maintenance depends, in the final analysis, upon co-operation.

We have formulated our programme for such co-operation into the following stages:

1. Each individual to apply scientific management to his own activities, individual and social.
2. Groups, such as industrial organisations, to apply scientific management to the group activity.
3. Trades to apply scientific management to the trade activity. This includes, ultimately, a reclassification and standardization of the trades, such as we have advocated in "Motion Study."[1] The trades must be classified according to the amount of skill involved in the motions used, and must then be standardized in order that the necessary training for succeeding in them can be given.
4. Industries to apply scientific management to the

[1] D. Van Nostrand Company, New York, pages 94–103.

entire industry, with co-operation between the various trades involved.

5. A national bureau of standardization to collect and formulate the data from all the industries into national standards.
6. An international bureau of standardization to collect national standards and to work for international co-operation.

America's immediate industrial position depends upon America's realisation of the need for conservation, as demonstrated by scientific management, and upon America's use of such means of conservation as scientific management offers.

America's ultimate industrial position depends upon America's realisation that the highest type of conservation includes co-operation.

Individuals, groups, trades, and industries have realised and are realising more and more, daily, that it is for the good of all that common practice be standardised and that improvements take place from the highest common standard. Nations have not yet come to any great realisation that this same principle applies to international relationships.

If America desires to gain and maintain leadership in industrial progress, she must be the advocate of industrial conservation and co-operation and must be the example of that readiness to derive and to share standards for which scientific management stands.

UNITS, METHODS, AND DEVICES OF MEASUREMENT UNDER SCIENTIFIC MANAGEMENT [1]

In any paper covering a subject of such scope as this, one can hope to do little more than outline the subject, but even for such an outline it is necessary to show at the outset the scheme of division, recognition, and interrelation of the functions of scientific management.

This can be done best by showing graphically two plans of management. The first of these (see Fig. 2) represents what is variously known as military or traditional management. Here each man is responsible to one man only above him, and is in charge of all those below him. Thus it is the custom for any man to come in contact with one man above him only, the line of authority being single and direct. Traditional management has been used for centuries in military organisations, and has also been used many

[1] Reprinted from *The Journal of Political Economy*, Vol. XXI.

times in religious organisations and political organisations. The division is by men, by grades of men, rather than by functions.

Because the division is by men, it is almost impossible to measure and standardise the duties of the positions. Any attempt at such measurement and standardisation makes clear the fact that the requirements of every position, with the exception of the most subordinate, demand men of a higher grade of development than the pay involved would justify. Moreover, as the supposed requirements of the positions are the result of guess or tradition rather than of measurement, successful standardisation would be not only impracticable, but impossible.

Fig. 3 represents the lines of authority in functional or scientific management. Here the division is by functions, the first functional division being the separation of the planning from the performing. Graphically, this separation is represented by the horizontal line. All functions above this line are of the planning, all functions below this line are of the performing. Note the functions shown on this chart, namely, four functions in the planning and four functions in

Fig. 2

Diagram illustrating the routes of authority under traditional type of management.

Fig. 3

Diagram illustrating the principle of functional or scientific management.

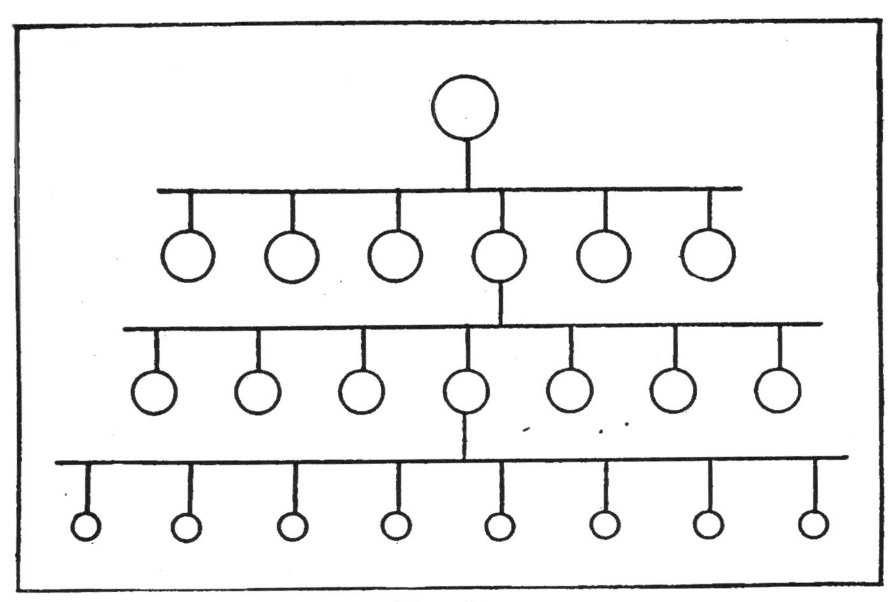

Fig. 2

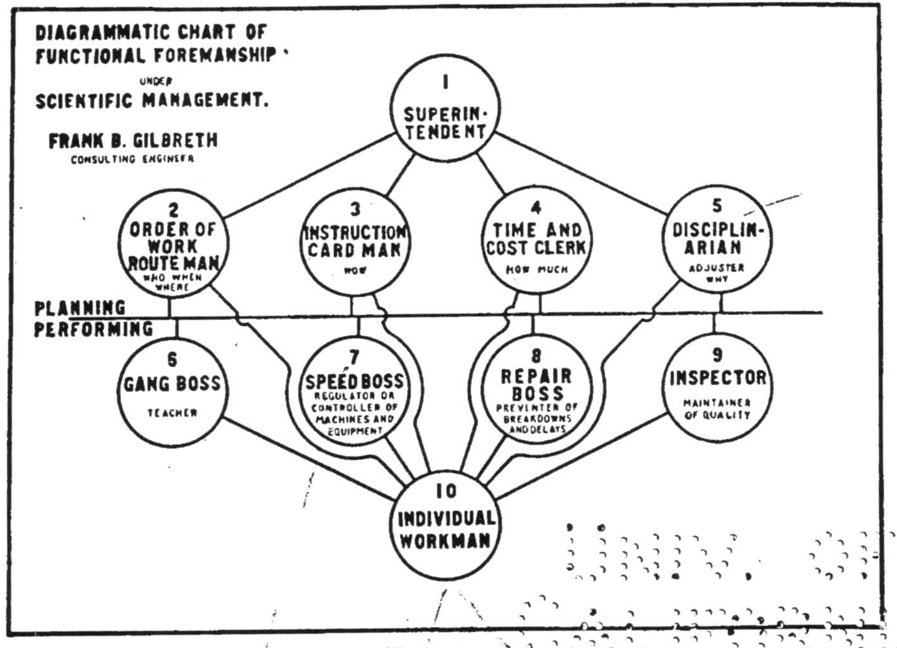

DIAGRAMMATIC CHART OF
FUNCTIONAL FOREMANSHIP
UNDER
SCIENTIFIC MANAGEMENT.
FRANK B. GILBRETH
CONSULTING ENGINEER
1
SUPERIN-TENDENT
2
ORDER OF WORK ROUTE MAN
WHO WHEN WHERE
3
INSTRUCTION CARD MAN
HOW
4
TIME AND COST CLERK
HOW MUCH
5
DISCIPLIN-ARIAN
ADJUSTER WHY
PLANNING
PERFORMING
6
GANG BOSS
TEACHER
7
SPEED BOSS
REGULATOR OR CONTROLLER OF MACHINES AND EQUIPMENT
8
REPAIR BOSS
PREVENTER OF BREAKDOWNS AND DELAYS
9
INSPECTOR
MAINTAINER OF QUALITY
10
INDIVIDUAL WORKMAN

Fig. 3

the performing. Note also their relation to each other, and to the individual worker. This chart shows one such worker represented by the lowest circle. There should be no objection to representing each individual worker by such a circle, but the relation of each such worker to those over him is the same. Hence, the lowest circle is typical.

It will be noted that the worker receives orders directly from eight different foremen. One might suggest, on observing this, that it has often been said that no man can serve two masters. This holds good to-day, even in scientific management. But under scientific management the worker does not "serve eight masters" nor eight functional foremen, but, on the other hand, he receives help from eight different foremen or teachers. In this way, his case is not very different from that of the student who receives instruction from eight different professors, in eight different studies.

The four functions in the planning department are represented by (2) route man and order-of-work man; (3) instruction cards; (4) time and cost; (5) disciplinarian. While we speak of each function as being represented by one person, as a matter of fact each function may include any number of individuals, according to the kind of work, and the number necessary to perform that function as to eliminate all possible waste. Each one of these four men of the four functions in the planning department is supreme in his respective function. All deal directly with the worker, and all deal directly with the four functional foremen who are in the performing department.

Of the *performing* department we have four functions represented by (7) gang boss; (8) speed boss; (9) repair boss; (10) inspector. These functions, like those of the planning department, are represented by as many men as the nature and amount of work justifies. All such representatives deal, as the chart indicates, directly both with all individuals in the planning department, and with each individual worker.

The fact that all divisions represented by this chart are made on the basis of the nature of the work that is to be done, makes possible units for measuring and standardising the duties of the man or men who hold the positions. The determining, grouping, and assigning of these duties is done by measurement; hence the resultant standardisation is successful. A statement of the duties of each function will make clear the amount of standardisation that is possible.

Route Man.— The duty of the route man (function No. 2) is to determine and plan in advance the path of each piece of material, worked and unworked, as it passes through the shop or as it is handled by each and every member of the organisation who has anything to do with it. He is to decide the three dimensions of the path, and the route that the material is to pass through, whether it is to go to the stores or into temporary storage stations, or directly through the shop as fast as the operations connected with it will permit. His function is not simply to look after the details of the moving; he must also determine the "when" and in many cases the "who" as well as the "where" Broadly, he determines the entire transportation career of the material. For example, in building operations, he would determine where the car was to be placed to be unloaded, where the material was to be unloaded, when it was to be moved into the building, and exactly what path it should follow across the floor, up elevators and to its final resting-place, and *who* should perform each operation.

Often the route man is able to simplify greatly the path of the materials, especially on large orders, by a rearrangement or routing of the machinery. We have had one case in our experience where it was cheaper, in a woodworking shop, to have the machinery placed on heavy pieces not attached to the floor, each machine operated by an individual motor, and to move the machinery, in order to accommodate the peculiarities of sequence of events of each particular order, when the order was large enough to warrant moving the machinery. The route man's duties, also, oftentimes involve determining a new path, ordering that machinery not used be removed, so that he can route his material by a more economical method. After he has determined the exact path by which the material shall be routed, he embodies his conclusions into process charts, route charts, and route sheets; these illustrate his orders graphically and chronologically and are worked out in detail by the instruction card department.

Instruction Cards.— It must not be supposed

that the instruction-card function consists merely of the work of writing out the instruction cards. This is the name of the function in general, and it may be performed by several men in different lines and of varying capacity in the instruction-card function; that is to say, the department or function may be divided into measurable units or subfunctions. It is the duty of the instruction-card function to work out in detail and to devise and construct an instruction card describing the method of least waste for each element of the route sheets which are made from the route charts. The instruction-card department furnishes in the greatest possible detail such directions as will show two different classes of men their duties, namely: (*a*) the worker, who must know how to perform the particular work shown on the instruction card; and (*b*) the functional foremen in the performing department, who must know exactly what they are to see that the worker does perform, and exactly what they are to teach the worker in order that he may so perform his work as to conform to the instruction card.

Time and Cost.—After the worker has performed his work, a return of the time that it took him to do his work, together with its cost, goes to the time and cost clerk (function No. 4) who calculates the pay-roll, including the bonuses, and the costs of each piece or subdivision of the work.

Disciplinarian.— The disciplinarian is the man who handles all matters in the entire organisation pertaining to discipline. He must be a broad-gauge man, who is able to keep peace in the organisation, to anticipate disagreements and misunderstandings and prevent them when possible, and to arbitrate or judge fairly such disagreements as do take place.

The functions in the performing department are now to be considered.

Gang Boss.— Function No. 7 is that of the teacher, still called "gang boss," as it was from that function that his work evolved. There may be many gang bosses in the performing department; in fact there are frequently five or more gang bosses of a single trade, with an over-gang boss in charge. Altogether there may be in this function gang bosses of twenty or thirty different trades, in fact of as many trades as are at work; or, possibly one gang boss might look after two or more trades. The gang boss under scientific management is not the "strong arm" type of man represented by the mate of the vessel of former days, who boasted that he could thrash any man in the entire crew, and often did so for no other reason than to prove his words. Instead he is a man who knows of the measuring methods of motion-study and time-study, and who can teach the worker the methods shown on the instruction card. In order to get his best work, and to enlist his zeal, it is usually necessary to pay him a bonus measured by the bonus paid each and every man under him who in turn earns his bonus; and a double bonus if every man in his gang earns the bonus. For example suppose the gang boss received $3.00 per day, and had twenty men working under him, he would be paid, say, in round numbers, 10 cents apiece for each man under him who received his bonus; and, if all twenty men received their bonus, he would receive a double bonus of 20 cents apiece for the entire gang.

It can readily be seen that such a plan of management as this will bring out co-operation as would no other plan; and it should be stated here emphatically that there is nothing that can permanently bring about results from scientific management, and the economies that it is possible to effect by it, unless the organisation is supported by the hearty co-operation of the men. Without this there is no scientific management.

Moreover, since the conditions which bring about the co-operation are measured and standardised, the result is stable. Co-operation without standardisation is a most unstable thing, likely to disappear at any moment with a change of the individuals supposed to co-operate.

Speed Boss.— Regardless of the popular impression as to his duties, the speed boss (function No. 8) does not speed up the men. In fact, he has very little to do with speeding men. His duty is to see that the machinery moves at the exact speed called for on the individual instruction card. It is obvious that there is some one speed that is more desirable than any other speed; for example, the speed of a buzz planer or a circular saw is very dangerous when it is too slow, while on the other hand, the speed of a fly-wheel of an engine is very dangerous when it is too fast. What is most desirable and safe is the speed that the instruction card man attempts to set on the instruction card, and it is the duty of the speed boss to see that the machinery runs at all times at exactly the prescribed speeds. He not only shows the worker how he can make his machine run at the speed called for, but, if there is a question as to its being possible to run at this speed, he must be prepared to teach the worker by doing the work himself, or provide a man who can comply with the requirements of the instruction card.

Repair Boss.— Function No. 9 is that of the repair boss. His duties consist principally in seeing that all machines are kept clean and in proper condition, and in carrying out repairs and over-haulings, such as are called for on instruction cards and in standing orders that are given to him at regular, predetermined intervals. In this way breakdowns are so far as possible avoided. The repair boss, however, must be a resourceful man, prepared, in case of emergency to jump in and repair any such breakdowns as may occur, even in the absence of precise directions or of instruction-card specifications.

Inspector.— Function No. 10 is that of the inspector. His duties are decidedly different from those of the inspector under the old type of management. For example, his inspection must result in prevention of error; in constructive criticism, not destructive criticism. His decisions are predetermined by measurable limits of error furnished both him and the workman by the instruction-card department.

Many times, under traditional management, the inspector comes around after the work is done, condemns it, and walks away, leaving it to others to see that the work is replaced to his satisfaction. Under scientific management the inspector is required to stand near the worker when he is handling a new piece of work for the first time, in order to see that the worker thoroughly understands his work as it progresses. Thus the first unit of the material is less likely to be spoiled. If the worker has a lot of, say, fifty pieces, the inspector inspects not only the first piece most carefully, to make sure that the worker knows exactly what he is to do, how he is to do it, and the quality and the prescribed tolerances of drawing and instruction card but also the surrounding conditions, equipment, and tools that the important features of maintenance of standards and standard conditions are enforced.

The Workman.—As for the individual worker, it will be seen that he does not receive merely an instruction card, telling him by units what he is to do, how he is to do it, how fast he is expected to do it, the prescribed quality of the work which must be done, and how much pay over and above his usual day's wages he will surely get if he does all that is called for on his instruction card. He receives also personal teaching. The gang boss acts as his teacher constantly; the speed boss he can call on at all times to assist him with the speeds; the repair boss co-operates with him to see that his machine is constantly kept in such repair that he can earn his bonus, and the inspector will also teach him at any time, and show him wherein he is making a deviation from the quality called for. Moreover, the functional foremen in the planning department are ready, at call, to explain their instructions. Thus he has every help that is possible, to enable him to earn the exceptionally high wages that are offered by this form of management. He is assured of the "square deal" from the foremen who are over him, and in case others whose work affects his are deviating from their measurable schedules, programmes, or conduct, he always has the same opportunity to appeal to the disciplinarian, that a foreman would have in case the worker was not doing his work as well as he could do it, or was not trying to co-operate with the other workers.

Having described briefly some of the many divisions and interrelations of the functions of scientific management and their foundation upon measurement, we are now ready to concentrate upon one, to show by a typical case how division of elements down to fundamental units may result in (*a*) determined units; (*b*) measured units; (*c*) devices of measurement. Let us take for a typical example two subfunctions of the instruction-card function, namely, motion-study and time-study, and carry them to micromotion-study.

Motion-study is a subfunction of function No. 3 of the planning department. Just as scientific management is divided into functions, so each function is divided into subfunctions, the basis of division being the same, i.e., duties, not men (see Fig. 3). Motion-study is related to all subfunctions of the instruction-card function, but is most closely related to time-study and to the determining of methods of least waste. It is related to time-study in that it determines what path a motion is to follow, while time-study determines how swiftly the path is to be traversed and the amount of rest required to overcome resulting fatigue. The two measure work and determine the best method by which the work can be done.

Motion-study, time-study, micromotion-study, fatigue-study, and cost-study are important measures of scientific management, by which the efficiency of each function and subfunction is determined, tested, and checked. The unit to be chosen for intensive study is determined by the amount of time and money that it is possible to save by the investigation. This unit is determined by the following method. The work selected is divided into natural subdivisions or cycles of performance. Each cycle is then subjected to motion study, to determine the best method to use in performing the work. This method is divided into the smallest practicable units. These units are timed. The timed units are then again subjected to motion study, for more intensive study of method. Subdivided motions result. These are again timed, and so the process proceeds until the further possible saving will no longer warrant further study, or the available appropriation of time or money is exhausted. The most efficient motions, as determined by the tests of motion-study and time-study are then synthesised into a method of least waste.

This outline of the steps in taking motion-study and time study is necessarily incomplete, lacking, as it does, discussion of the selection of the observer, the observed worker, and many other elements of scientific management.

As for the particular device by which the measurements are made, the choice depends mainly on the equipment available. Standards have been improved even by merely timing the work by counting, where no timing devices were at hand. Excellent work had been done with stop watches. But we advocate the use of micromotion-study in all work demanding precision. Micromotion-study consists of recording the speed simultaneously with a two or three dimensional path of motions by the aid of cinematograph pictures of a worker at work and a specially designed clock that shows divisions of time so minute as to indicate a different time of day in each picture in the cinematograph film. Through micromotion-study

FIG. 4

Reaction test of Miss Anna Gold, who afterward became National Amateur Champion Typist by winning the contest at Chicago, 1916.

FIG. 5

Miss Hortense Stollnitz,— who afterward became International Amateur Champion, equalling the professional record of 137 words per minute net, and exceeding all previous records with 147 words per minute gross,— changing paper in the machine.

FIG. 6

Miss Stollnitz' finger motions while writing at her fastest speed. These pictures were taken at the rate of 115 exposures per second, and can be studied with special apparatus as continuous motions at the rate of eight per second.

Fig. 4

Fig. 5

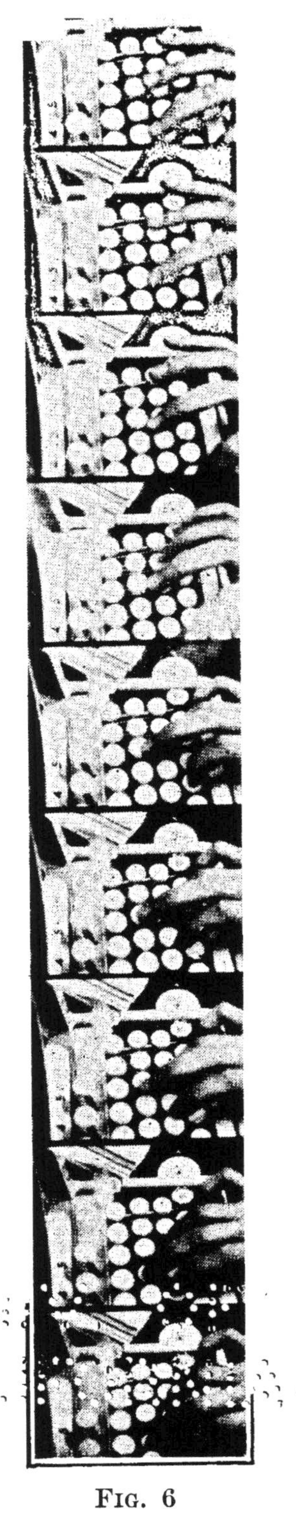

Fig. 6

not only is the measurement more accurate than it could possibly be through any other method, but also the records are so complete, permanent, and accessible that they may be studied at any time and place by any one. The advantages of this in standardising work, and most especially in teaching workers, are obvious.

The result of measurement, as outlined above, is standards synthesised from measured ultimate units of the workers' manual motions.

Morris Llewellyn Cooke, Director of the Philadelphia Department of Public Works, in *Bulletin 5* of the Carnegie Foundation for the Advancement of Teaching, created for the word "standard" a definition which is itself "standard" in the scientific management sense. He said

> A standard under modern scientific management is simply a carefully thought-out method of performing a function, or carefully drawn specifications covering an implement or some article of stores or of product. The idea of perfection is not involved in standardisation. The standard method of doing anything is simply the best method that can be devised at the time the standard is drawn. Standard specifications for materials simply cover all the points of possible variation which it is possible to cover at the time the specifications are drawn.

Improvements in standards are wanted and adopted whenever and wherever they are found. There is absolutely nothing in standardisation to preclude innovation. But to protect standards from changes which are not in the direction of improvement, certain safeguards are erected. These safeguards protect standards from change for the sake of change. All that is demanded under modern scientific management is that a proposed change in a standard must be scrutinised as carefully as the standard was scrutinised prior to its adoption, and further that this work be done by experts as competent to do it as were those who originally framed the standard. Standards adopted and protected in this way produce the best that is known at any one time. Standardisation practised in this way is a constant invitation to experimentation and improvement.

This experimentation and improvement are done by time and motion study *before* the standards are made. Thus the resulting standard is in so far perfected that only the invention of a new device will make a change in the standard necessary. The fact that such devices are often the result of the motion study also assists in making the standards that are incorporated from the completed study more permanent.

As was well shown by Mr. John G. Aldrich, in a paper read before the American Society of

Mechanical Engineers, in December, 1912, the waste motions eliminated by such measured standardising can scarcely be overestimated. This has been demonstrated in many lines of activity. The standard toolroom, the standard assembly packet and bench for assembling, the standard desk in the planning department — these are but illustrations of the application of this principle. And it is not necessary that the illustrations be drawn from the field of shopwork. It has been applied to many of the outdoor trades. We are now co-operating with famous surgeons in the study of the elementary motions used in surgery, and we are investigating the muscular activity that underlies the "singing tone" of the skilled musician, to mention two recent invasions of the fields of science and art.

There will be those who will say that no such theory, methods, or devices can ever supplant the need and usefulness of the first-class mechanic or the genius in the trades, arts, and professions. With this we humbly agree. But even two geniuses in the same work may differ greatly in their methods as a whole; and isolating and examining the ultimate units of their work may show that motions made by one of the geniuses may be found absent, and unnecessary, in the work of the other. A synthesis of the best of the units of methods of each would present a method better than any arrived at by the spontaneity of any one genius, no matter how great. Surely the presentation of the best method, however discovered, must be of the greatest value to all below the grade of best.

Meantime, all workers are sharing in the savings made possible by the elimination of waste. They are being trained in habits of least wasteful motions, and are becoming more efficient both in their working and in their non-working hours. They learn to "think in elementary motions," and to submit their activities in all lines to the tests of motion and time study.

The great need now is for more efficient co-operation, that work done by one investigator may not be needlessly repeated by another. Through such co-operation only can come the savings that will allow of refinements of the units, methods, and devices of measurement, and that will result in progress that is definite, constant, and lasting.

MOTION STUDY AS AN INDUSTRIAL OPPORTUNITY[1]

There is no waste of any kind in the world that equals the waste from needless, ill-directed, and ineffective motions, and their resulting unnecessary fatigue. Because this is true, there is no industrial opportunity that offers a richer return than the elimination of needless motions, and the transformation of ill-directed and ineffective motions into efficient activity.

This country has been so rich in human and material resources, that it is only recently that the importance of waste elimination has come to be realised. The material element received the first consideration, and in the comparatively few years during which the subject has received attention, an enormous amount has been done to conserve natural resources, to economise in the use of materials, and to utilise the by-products of industrial processes.

The human element is now receiving long-delayed attention. Vocational training, vocational

[1] Reprinted from "The Annals" of the American Academy of Political and Social Science.

guidance, better placement, and better working conditions have become subjects for serious consideration in all parts of this country and of the world. Savings in human energy are resulting from these investigations, but the greatest saving in time, in money, and in energy will result when the motions of every individual, no matter what his work may be, have been studied and standardised.

Such studies have already been made in many trades, and have resulted in actual savings that prove that the results of the practice confirm the theory. In laying brick, the motions used in laying a single brick were reduced from eighteen to five,— with an increase in output of from one hundred and twenty brick an hour to three hundred and fifty an hour and with a reduction in the resulting fatigue. In folding cotton cloth, twenty to thirty motions were reduced to ten or twelve, with the result that instead of one hundred and fifty dozen pieces of cloth, four hundred dozen were folded, with no added fatigue. The motions of a girl putting paper on boxes of shoe polish were studied. Her methods were changed only slightly, and where she had been doing twenty-four boxes in forty seconds, she did twenty-four in twenty seconds, with less effort. Similar studies have cut down the motions not only of men and women in other trades but also of surgeons, of nurses, of office workers; in fact, of workers in every type of work studied

Motion study consists of dividing work into the most fundamental elements possible; studying these elements separately and in relation to one another; and from these studied elements, when timed, building methods of least waste.

To cite a specific example: The assembly of a machine is the piece of work under consideration. The existing method of assembling the machine is recorded in the minutest detail. Each element of the assembly is then tested,— the method used in handling the element being compared with other possible methods. In this way, the most efficient elements of an assembly are determined; and these elements are combined into a method of assembly that, because it is the result of actual measurement, is worthy to become a standard. Such an assembly is that of the braider, manufactured by the New England Butt Company. As a result of motion studies made upon this, where eighteen braiders had been assembled by one man in a day, it now becomes possible to assemble sixty-six braiders per man per day, with no increase in fatigue.

The accurate measurement involved in getting results like this includes three elements. We must determine, first, the units to be measured; second, the methods to be used; and, third, the devices to be used.

The unit of measurement must be one that of itself will reduce cost, and should be as small as the time and money that can be devoted to the investigation warrants. The smaller the unit, the more intensive the study required.

The methods and devices to be used are also determined largely by the question of cost. Naturally, those methods and devices are preferable which provide least possibility of errors of observation. Such errors have been classified as of two kinds: First, errors due to instruments; and, second, errors due to the personal bias of the observer. The newer methods of making motion studies and time studies by the use of the micromotion method and the chronocyclegraph method exclude such errors. Fortunately, through an

Fig. 7

Automatic Micromotion Study with vertical penetrating screen in the plane of the motions.

Fig. 8

Multiple use of film reducing cost of time and motion study while retaining accuracy and permanence of the detailed record.

Fig. 9

Autoteletime study for recording motions at a great distance and the position of the finger of the michronometer less than thirty feet away.

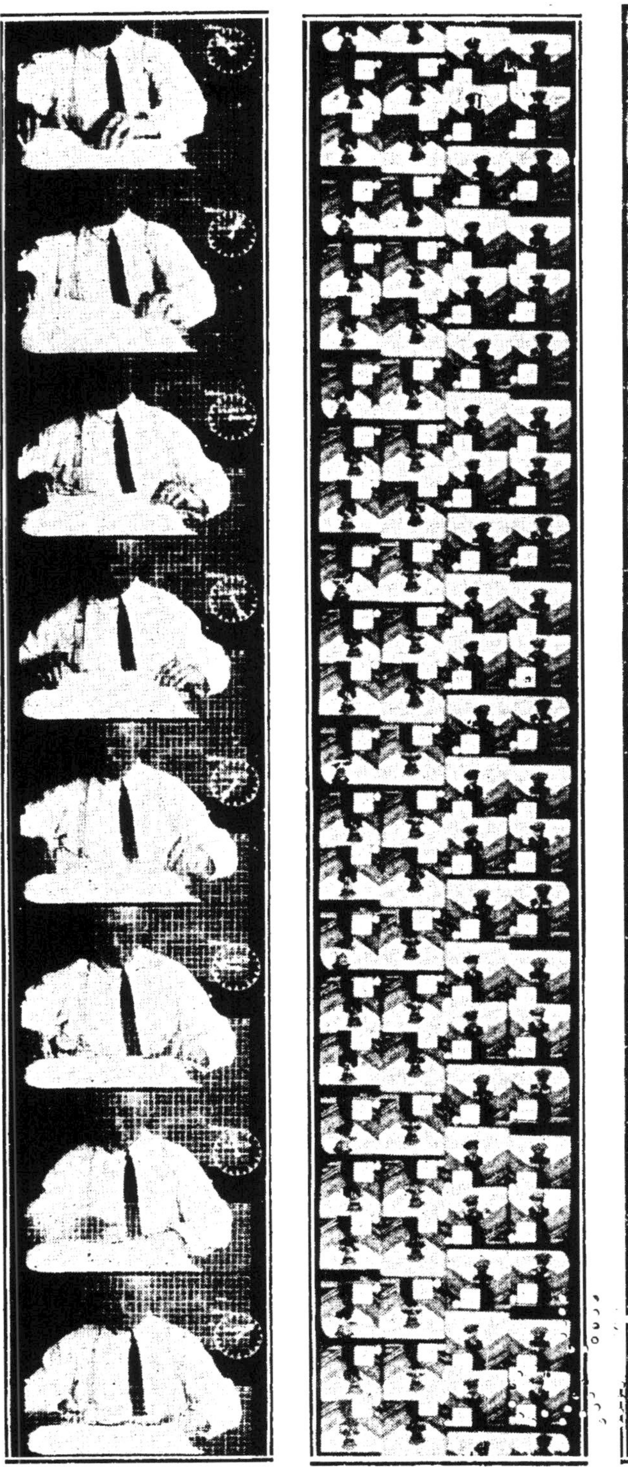

FIG. 7 FIG. 8

FIG. 9

improvement and cheapening of the devices, it is now possible to make accurate records of motions, even when no great outlay for the study can be afforded.

The micro-motion method of making motion studies consists of recording motions by means of a motion picture camera, a clock that will record different times of day in each picture of a motion picture film, a cross-sectioned background, and other devices for assisting in measuring the relative efficiency and wastefulness of motions.

Suppose the process of assembly before cited is being micro-motion studied: The assembler is placed before the cross-sectioned background; the micro-motion clock is placed where it will record in the picture, yet not disturb the worker; near it is another clock which serves as a check on the accuracy of the special clock. The assembler, who has been rated a skilled worker under the old method, naturally does the best work possible, since a permanent record is being made of his performance. The observer operates the motion picture camera, which, however, allows him freedom to observe the assembly process continually, and to note possibilities for improvement.

From the data on the film and the observations of the observer, can be formulated an improved method. The standard method is seldom derived from the work of one observed worker only. It has been noted that *the ideal method seldom lies in the consecutive acts of any one individual;* therefore, many workers are observed before the final standard is deduced.

These micro-motion records give all the data required except the continuous path of a cycle of motions. This lack is supplied by the chronocyclegraph method. The chronocyclegraph method of making motion study consists of fastening tiny electric-light bulbs to the fingers of the operator, or to any part of the operator or of the material whose motion path it is desired to study. If it is merely the orbit of the motion that is to be observed, a photograph is made of the moving part to which the light is attached, during the time that this part is performing the operation. If the direction, relative time, and relative speed are to be noted, the path of light, through controlled interruption of the circuit, is made to consist of dots or dashes, or a combination of the two, with single pointed ends,— the point showing the direction. Through the micro-motion studies and the chronocyclegraph studies, then, the expert formulates the standard method. It is important to note the changes which the installation of a standard method implies. This method consists of improved motions, and implies, first, changes in surroundings, equipment, and tools; and, second, changes in the type of worker assigned to do the work.

During the motion study of the assembly, it was found that more efficient motions could be made if the machine assembled was placed on a special table, which could be turned on its side and transformed into a lower table, after the base group of the machine had been assembled. It was also found that speed was gained and fatigue eliminated, when the parts of the machine were arranged in an obvious sequence on a vertical packet.[1] These devices were immediately supplied at little cost and with great result in saving. Through these devices, and the other changes made by motion study, it became possible to accomplish nearly three and one-half times

1 For description of the original motion study packet see "Bricklaying System," Chap. VIII.

as much assembly as had previously been done. Such changes are typical, and it is typical that the inventions *result from* the motion study.

As for the type of individual suited to the work, — the simplification of the process and the reduction of the motions to habits often make it possible to utilise workers with less initiative and skill, assigning the more skilled workers to a higher type of work. In the case cited of the assembly, the original assemblers were retained and enabled to do much more work with less fatigue. It has also been possible to train inexperienced men to assemble in much less time and with less effort than was formerly the case.

The result of the introduction of motion standards is an increase in output and wages, and an accompanying decrease in cost and fatigue. The decreased cost and the increased wages both depend, of course, on the increased output. The output is increased, because the motions used to make any one unit of the output are less in number and more efficient in results. The average cost of output increase is sufficient not only to provide for the higher wages necessary to induce the workers to do the work in the manner prescribed, and to enjoy doing it, but, also, to allow of at least enough profit to the management to cover the cost of the investigations that resulted in the standard.

The *quality* of the output is maintained through a new type of inspection, which considers not only the output itself, but the elements,— material and human,— which result in that output. Nothing is a higher guarantee of quality than insistence on a standard method.

Along with the laboratory investigations from which motion study standards are derived, goes a general campaign to arouse every individual in the organisation to think in terms of elements of motions. Such simple office equipment as pencil holders are motion studied, and every member of the organisation is encouraged to observe and record his own motions in performing the most elementary of operations. Motion study may be carried on with no devices, and every one is expected to know how to make at least the preliminary investigations. In this way, the spirit of motion economy grows throughout the entire plant, with a consequent elimination of waste motions and a growing interest in the more scientific methods of motion study.

What, now, are the results of this motion study upon the individual men doing the work, upon the factory group, upon the industrial world, and upon society at large? The men themselves become more efficient. They become specialists,—skilled workers. They learn the motion-study method of attack, and are thus more fit to undertake any type of work. They learn to think in elementary motions, and to eliminate waste in every activity of their lives.

The increased output of each individual worker does not result in the employment of less men in the plant. The transference of skill that maintenance of standards implies, means that many teachers are needed. These come, naturally, from the ranks of the skilled workers. The planning that is necessary is also usually done by workers promoted to the planning department. At present, at least, the demand for men trained under motion study is far larger than the supply; it will be for years to come,—certainly until the increased output results in the increased demand which is its inevitable consequence.

The industrial situation is bettered through the

general spread of the ideas of waste elimination, and through the practical application of its principles in whatever relations those trained under it may enter. How far this influence upon the industries will extend will depend entirely upon the amount of work done by individuals, and upon their co-operation. At present, many individuals are engaged in, or are at least interested in, motion study and waste elimination. But there is not the proper degree of co-operation. Such co-operation can only come as motion study becomes a matter of interest to society at large. The whole social group is already being affected by the results of motion study. One typical result is the gradual filling in of the gap between the school and the plant. An intensive study of motions is proving that there are far greater likenesses in trades, and even professions, on the mechanical side, than we have ever believed possible. The demand of the industrial world will be more and more for young workers trained to be finger-wise, with a knowledge of the fundamentals of motion economy, and with an understanding of the relationship between efficient motions and success in the industries.

The industrial world is becoming more and more definite in its requirements for industrial training. This is making it possible for all types of schools to give their pupils a training which enables them to fit into working conditions without the customary, preliminary jolt, and months and years of adjustment. The training required is so general, yet so definite, that it may well prove an important part of the training of every young man or woman, whether or not he goes ultimately into the industries. This training is being given not only in the technical schools and in the trade schools but also to some extent, at least, in the ordinary public schools. It consists of making every pupil, to as great an extent as possible, "finger-wise"; that is, of training his muscles so that they respond easily and quickly to demands for skilled work. With this training goes an appreciation of the importance of such "finger training," and of its relation to motion economy. The pupils are also given an appreciation of the problems of industry, and of the relation of these problems to social development.

An effect of motion study in the industries upon society is its influence toward spreading the belief that real efficiency considers and conserves the human element;[1] that it makes fatigue study imperative; and that its fundamental idea is conservation, not exploitation.

The great need to-day, as in all fields where progress is to be made, is education. The community as a whole must be educated as to the importance of motion study, and as to the possibility of every man and woman making such motion study to some extent for himself. The technical press and the press generally are doing much to spread these ideas. Much is also being done by the colleges that are studying and teaching the subject. Such wide-spread education is absolutely necessary before we can hope for the reclassification and standardisation of the existing trades, which is a necessary future step. The trades must be reclassified, according to the amount of skill involved in the motions used; and must then be standardised in order that the necessary training for entering them and succeeding in them can be given. As an example of reclassifying a trade, we would recommend, for example, for brick work, five classes:

1 See "Fatigue Study," p. 10, Sturgis & Walton, New York.

Class A.—Ornamental and exterior face brick and moulded terra cotta.

Class B.—Interior face tiers that do not show at completion, where strong, plumb, and straight work only is needed.

Class C.—Filling tiers where strength only is needed.

Class D.—Putting fountain trowels and brick packs on the wall near the place, and in the manner where the other three classes can reach them with greatest economy of motion.

Class E.—Pack loaders, brick cullers, and stage builders.

The pay of the A and B classes should be considerably higher than is customary for bricklayers. The pay of the C, D, and E classes should be lower than is customary for bricklayers, but much higher than the pay of labourers. This classification will raise the pay of all five classes higher than they could ever obtain in the classes that they would ordinarily work in under the present system, yet the resulting cost of the labour on brickwork would be much less, and each class would be raised in its standing and educated for better work and higher wages.

In the case of brickwork this new classification is a crying necessity, as the cost of brickwork must be reduced to a point where it can compete with concrete. Improvements in making, methods of mixing, transporting, and densifying concrete in the metal moulds of to-day have put the entire brickwork proposition where it can be used for looks only, because for strength, imperviousness, quickness of construction, lack of union labour troubles, and low cost, brickwork cannot compete with concrete under present conditions.

Having subclassified the trades, the second step is to standardise them.

And both classification and standardisation demand motion study.

The other great need, besides education, is, then, a national bureau of standards, where work done in motion study can be collected, classified, and put into such form that it will be available to every one. There is an enormous waste, at present, from repeating investigations along the same lines of work. There is not only the waste from the actual repetition involved, but also the fact that the time utilised in doing work already done could, instead, be devoted to original work, that is sadly needed.

It is the work of the United States Government to establish such a Bureau of Standardisation of Mechanical Trades. The standards there derived and collected would be public property, and original investigators could invent from these standards upwards. Most important of all, perhaps, these standards would furnish the ideal means for teaching or transferring skill to the young workers who desire to enter a trade.

The reclassification of the trades and the Bureau of Standardisation are, then, the two great needs for motion study development. But these will come only when the individuals interested apply motion study to their own work, and show willingness to co-operate with others.

The industrial opportunity afforded by motion study is not, then, some great future opportunity of which we dream, or some remote and inaccessible opportunity for which we must collectively strive. It is an opportunity ready, here and now, to be grasped by each one of us individually,—and it is the greatest industrial opportunity that this century affords.

MOTION STUDY AND TIME STUDY INSTRUMENTS OF PRECISION [1]

The greatest waste in the world comes from needless, ill-directed, and ineffective motions. These motions are unnecessary and preventable. Their existence in the past was excusable, because there was no knowledge of how to dispense with them. That excuse no longer obtains. The methods and devices of waste elimination are known and are being constantly used. But the knowledge of how to make these great world-wide economies is being disseminated at an astonishingly slow pace.

This paper is for the purpose of disseminating such knowledge, particularly as to the devices that are used for making the measurements that enable us to eliminate waste.

In the science of management, as in all other sciences, progress that is to be definite and lasting depends upon the accuracy of the measure-

1 Presented at the International Engineering Congress.

ments that are made. There are three elements to every measurement:

1. The unit measured.

2. The method of measurement.

3. The device by which the measurement is made.

It is here our aim to show the development of the devices of measurement, that is, of instruments of precision that apply to one branch of the new type of management, namely, to motion study and its related time study.

The fundamental idea of the new type of management that has been variously called "Scientific Management," or "Measured Functional Management," is that it is based upon the results of accurate measurement. This fundamental idea has been derived as follows: Each operation to be studied is analysed into the most elementary units possible. These units are accurately measured, and, as the results of the measurement, the efficient units only are combined into a new method of performing the work that is worthy to become a standard.

Dr. Taylor, the great pioneer in time study, and his co-worker, Mr. S. E. Thompson, have clearly defined their conception of time study as "the process of analysing an operation into its elementary operations, and observing the time required to perform them." Time study has to do, then, fundamentally, with the measurement of units of time.

Now motion study has to do with the selection, invention, and substitution of the motions and their variables that are to be measured. Both accurate time study and motion study require instruments of precision that will record mechanically, with the least possible interference from the human element, in permanent form, exactly what motions and results occur. For permanent use the records must be so definite, distinct, and simple that they may be easily and immediately used, and lose none of their value or helpfulness when old, forgotten, or not personally experienced by their user.

There have undoubtedly been some vague motion studies and guess-work times studies made as far back as historical records are available, particularly in the arts of warfare. The importance of rhythm, for example, which is one of the fundamentals in motion study, was recognised in the

Assyrian and Babylonian pictorial records which perpetuate the methods of their best managers, as examination of photographs of such records in our possession will plainly show. Babbage, Coulomb, Adam Smith,— all recognised the importance of the time element in industrial operations, for the purpose of obtaining methods of greatest output, but not methods of least waste. It was not, however, until Dr. Taylor suggested timing the work periods separately from the rest periods that the managers tried to find accurate time-measuring devices.

It is not always recognised that some preliminary motion study and time study can be done without the aid of any accurate devices. It is even less often recognised that such work, when most successful, is usually done by one thoroughly conversant with, and skilled in, the use of the most accurate devices. In other words, it is usually advisable in studying an operation to make all possible improvements in the motions used and to comply broadly with the laws of motion study before recording the operation, except for the preliminary record that serves to show the state of the art from which the investigation started. However, in order to make a great and lasting success of this work, one must have studied motions and measured them until his eye can follow paths of motions and judge lengths of motions, and his timing sense, aided by silent rhythmic counting, can estimate times of motion with surprising accuracy. Sight, hearing, touch, and kinesthetic sensations must all be keenly developed. With this training and equipment, a motion- and time-study expert can obtain preliminary results without devices, that, to the untrained or the uninformed, seem little short of astounding. When the operation has received its preliminary revision and is ready for the accurate measurements that lead to actual standardisation and the teaching that follows, devices of precise measurement become imperative for methods of least waste that will stand the test of time.

Early workers in time study made use of such well-known devices as the clock, the watch, the stop-watch, and various types of stop-watches attached to a specially constructed board or imitation book. Through the use of these it became possible to record short intervals of time, subject, of course, always to the personal error. The objection to the use of these methods and devices is their variation from accuracy, due to the human element. This is especially true of the use of the stop-watch, where the reaction time of the observer is an element constantly affecting the accuracy of the records. But the greatest loss and defect of personally observed and recorded times is that they do not show the attending conditions of the varying surroundings, equipment and tools that cause the differences in the time records, and give no clue to causes of shortest or quickest times.

As for motion study, Marey, with no thought of motion study in our present use of the term in his mind, developed, as one line of his multitudinous activities, a method of recording paths of motions, but never succeeded in his effort to record direction of motions photographically.

Being unable to find any devices anywhere such as the work of our motion study required, the problem that presented itself, then, to us who needed and desired instruments of precision, applicable to our motion study and to our time study, was to invent, design and construct devices that would overcome lacks in the early and existing methods. It was necessary to dispense with the human element and its attending errors and limitations. We needed devices to record the direction as well as the path or orbits of motions, and to reduce the cost of obtaining all time study and motion study data. These were needed not only from the scientific standpoint, but also from the standpoint of obtaining full cooperation of the mechanics and other workers. Many of these had, as a class, become suspicious of time study taken secretly by those who, they thought, did not know enough about the practical features of the trade to take the time study properly, and could not prove that the times were right after putting them on paper. Here was absolute pioneer work to be done in inventing devices that would record times, paths, and directions of motions simultaneously. With the older time study devices there was no way of recording accurately either the unit timed or the controlling surrounding conditions. The "elementary units" were groups of motions. They were elementary only with relation to the stop-watch, with which it is impossible to record accurately the time of an element of a motion, since it takes two decisions and two motions to press the stop-watch. These "groups of motions" were sometimes described at greater or less length, the accuracy of the description depending upon the power of observation of the recorder and the detail with which the time at his disposal, his willingness and his ability to observe, permitted him to set down his observations.

Through our earliest work in making progress records we recognised the necessity of recording time and conditions accurately and simultaneously, the records being made by dated photographs. This method was particularly applicable in construction work,[1] where progress pictures taken at frequent intervals present accurate records of the surroundings, equipment and tools that affect records of output of various stages of development.

In making more intensive studies of certain trades, such as shovelling, concrete work, and bricklaying, we found it advantageous to photograph the various positions in which the hands, arms, feet, and other parts of the body involved

[1] See "Concrete System," Engineering News Publishing Co., New York.

in the operations were placed, and to record the time taken in moving from one position to another by one method, as related to the time taken in moving from the same first to the same second position by another method.[1] Our intensive study of bricklaying, which grew out of an appreciation of the unique history, present practice and doubtful future of this trade, led us to a more intensive study of the problems of motion and time study in general.[2] Bricklaying will always be the most interesting of all examples to us, for one reason, among others, that it was the first trade to use the principle of duplicate, interchangeable parts system of construction; had had six thousand known years of practice in all countries; and was, therefore, a comparatively finished art, but not a science, when we undertook to change it by means of motion study.

Fortunately, we are now able to use the motion picture camera with our speed clock, and other accessories, as a device for recording elements of motion and their corresponding times, simultane-

1 See "Motion Study," D. Van Nostrand Co., New York City.

2 See "Bricklaying System," Myron C. Clark Publishing Co., Chicago.

ously. Our latest microchronometer records intervals of time down to any degree of accuracy required. We have made, and used, in our work of motion study investigations of hospital practice and surgery, one that records times to the millionth of an hour. This is designed for extremely accurate work, but can be adjusted to intervals of any length desired, as proves most economical or desirable for the type of work to be investigated.

Having completed our microchronometer, we proceeded as follows: The microchronometer was placed in the photographic field near the operator and his working equipment, and against a cross-sectioned background or in a cross-sectioned field, and at a cross-sectioned work bench or table. The operator then performed the operation according to the prescribed method, while the motion-picture camera recorded the various stages of the operation and the position of the hand on the microchronometer simultaneously. Thus, on the motion picture film we obtain intermittent records of the paths, the lengths, the directions, and the speeds of the motions, or the times accompanying the motions, these records all being simultaneous; and the details of the conditions of the surroundings that are visible to the eye are recorded without the failings of memory. This was a distinct step in advance, but we realised that there was a lack in the records. It was difficult, even for one especially trained and experienced to visualise the exact path of a motion, and it was not possible to measure the length with precision from the observations of the motion picture film alone, as there is no summary or recapitulation of all the motions of a cycle or operation in any one picture. To overcome this lack we invented the cyclegraph method of recording motions. This consists of attaching a small electric light to the hand or other moving part of the person or machine under observation. The motion is recorded on an ordinary photographic film or plate. Upon observing our very first cyclegraph records, we found that we had attained our desire, and that the accurate path taken by the motion stood before us in two dimensions. By taking the photographic record stereoscopically, we were able to see this path in three dimensions, and to obtain what we have called the stereocyclegraph. This showed us the path of the motion in all three dimensions; that is, length, breadth, and depth. It did not, however, contain the time element. This time element is of great importance not only for comparative or "relative" time, but also for exact times. This time element is obtained by putting an interrupter in the light circuit, that causes the light to flash at an even rate at a known number of times per second. This gives a line of time spots in the picture instead of a continuous cyclegraph light line. Counting the light spots tells the time consumed.

The next step was to show the direction of the motions. To do this it was necessary to find the right combination of volts and amperes for the light circuit and the thickness of filament for the lamp, to cause quick lighting and slow extinguishing of the lamp. This right combination makes the light spots pointed on their latest, or forward, ends. The points, thus, like the usual symbol of arrow heads, show the direction. The result was, then, of course, finally, stereochronocyclegraphs showing direction. These act not only as accurate records of the motions and times, but also serve as admirable teaching devices.

Wire models of cyclegraphs and chronocyclegraphs of the paths and the times of motions are now constructed that have a practical educational value besides their importance as scientific records. These models are particularly useful as a step in teaching visualisation of paths by photographs alone, later.

Our latest apparatus in the field of recording devices apparently fulfils all present requirements of the time- and motion-study experts and their assistants and the teachers who are now devoting their lives to the transference of skill and experience from those who have it to those who have not.[1]

We have also devised and used many special kinds of apparatus; for example, devices for recording absolute continuity of motion paths and times, doing away with the slight gaps in the record that occur between one picture and the next on the cinematograph film, due to the interval of time when the film is moving, to get in place for the next exposure. To overcome this objection we have a double cinematograph, that one part may record while the other moves from

[1] See "Primer of Scientific Management," D. Van Nostrand Co., New York.

one exposure to the next. In this way we get a continuous record of the operation. There have been occasional objections to all methods of making time and motion studies that involve the presence of an observer. Some of these have come from those working on what they consider their own secret processes, who object to having any observer record what they are doing, believing that the time study man is obtaining knowledge of their skill and giving them no information in return. Others have come from those who have seen or heard "secret time study" and "watchbook time study," and who regard all observers as spies because of general lack of understanding and co-operation; and there are some instances where they are right. For such cases we have designed an automicromotion study, which consists of an instantaneous modification of the standard micromotion apparatus, and also the autostereochronocyclegraph apparatus. This enables the operator to take accurate time study of himself. He can start the apparatus going and stop it from where he works, with one motion of his finger or foot. This invention supplies every possible requirement and feature for time and

FIG. 10

Prof. Frank E. Sanborn recording times and paths of his own motions by the automicromotion device.

FIG. 10

motion study processes, except the help and advice of a properly qualified observer, or the annoyance of having one not fitted by training, experience, or natural qualities to co-operate.

There is not space in this paper for a discussion of the educational features of observations made with these devices, or of their influence upon the new and much needed science of fatigue study, or of their general psychological significance.[1] It is only necessary to emphasise their adaptability, flexibility, and relation to economy. We have here a complete set of inexpensive, light, durable apparatus, adaptable to any type of work and to any type of observer or self-observation. It consists of systematically assembled units that may be so combined as to meet any possible working condition. Through a specially devised method of using the same motion picture film over and over again, up to sixteen times, and through a careful study of electrical equipment and of various types of time spot interrupters, we have been enabled to cut down the cost of making time and motion study, until now the most accurate type of studies, involving no human equation in

1 See "Fatigue Study," Sturgis & Walton, New York.

the record, can be made at less cost than the far less accurate stop-watch study. This time study and motion study data can be used when it is "cold." No specially gifted observer, combined with the most willing and efficient recorder, can compete with it for observing and recording facts. It does not depend upon a human memory to "give up" its facts. It is usable at any time and forever, after it is once taken. Naturally, the requirements for refinement and the special set-ups to be used in any case must be determined after some study of the case in hand.

There are now available, therefore, instruments of precision fitted to make measurements as fine as the most exact science demands,— economical enough to make both immediate and ultimate savings, and that meet the demands of the most exacting industrial progressive. When the time and motion study is taken with such instruments of precision, there are still other by-products that are of more value than the entire cost of the time and motion studies.[1]

[1] See "Time Study; a Factor in the Science of Obtaining Methods of Least Waste."

See "Psychology of Management," Sturgis & Walton, New York.

CHRONOCYCLEGRAPH MOTION DEVICES FOR MEASURING ACHIEVEMENT[1]

The great need of this age is the conservation of the human element.

It will be the aim of this paper to show:

1. That the human element can be more efficiently utilised, and conserved to a greater degree, by the elimination of useless, ineffective and ill-directed motions.
2. That permanent elimination of such motions necessitates standardising the motions used in any activity.
3. That standardisation demands accurate devices for measuring achievement.
4. That chronocyclegraph motion devices measure achievement accurately, and thus provide for standardisation and, ultimately, for motion economy.

Stupendous as the financial loss to the entire world is, on account of the great war that is now

[1] A paper presented at the Second Pan-American-Congress at Washington, D. C., January 3, 1916.

being waged in many countries, and affecting all countries, it is as nothing compared to the world's loss of the human element. This is not only a loss that is being felt by this generation, but it is a loss that will be felt for many generations to come. It is, therefore, a great world problem, demanding the attention of all of us, to conserve and utilise humanity in every way possible. This problem has two aspects. The first is the utilisation of those directly affected by the war, either by being crippled or maimed through some injury received in the war, or by being forced to become productive members of the community through loss or crippling of the earning members of the family caused by the war. The second is the more efficient utilisation of all other members of the community, in order to make up, as far as possible, for the loss in productive power of individuals either killed or rendered in some way less efficient by the war.

The need for economy in the expenditure of human effort is not new. Even in the days of the Pharaohs there was the realisation that every ounce of strength of the worker was of value, as is plainly shown by photographs of the ancient carvings and other records of their industrial practice. There was, unfortunately, in those times little or no appreciation of the humanitarian side, of the need for conserving the worker for his own happiness and for the ultimate good of the race or the country. The practice was to extract every ounce of effort from the worker in the shortest amount of time possible, taking little account of the amount that the worker's life was shortened by the process. With the ages has come an appreciation of the greater benefit, not only to the individuals in society, but to society as a whole, to be derived by prolonging the life of the worker and increasing the number of happiness minutes that he enjoys. With the spread and growth of the movement for conserving material things, such as forests, mines and other natural resources, and the utilisation of the sources of energy, such as water power, has come an appreciation of the field for conservation of the human element. With the growth of the science of management, and the emphasis laid on motion study and fatigue study, has come an appreciation of the methods that may best be used to effect this conservation. Now, with the enormous need, has come the realisation that practice of this conservation should be started immediately, and maintained permanently, or, at least, for generations to come, if the world ever expects to recover from its stupendous and almost incalculable war loss.

"Economy" has become the watchword of the day, and it is an excellent watchword, but the practice of *unstudied* economy is apt to lead to serious economic disturbances. The first step in rational economy consists of investigating the relation between economy and waste elimination. It is necessary to realise the need to eliminate the useless and the need to utilise to the fullest capacity everything that is of use. This requires

1. The determination as to what is useless and as to what is useful.
2. The determination as to the most efficient method of utilising the useful.

That is to say, it requires accurate measurement applicable to activity. The problem is not simple, for along with the activity and its resulting achievement and output comes the fatigue accumulated by the worker while doing the work, and fatigue is a subject concerning which, as yet, little is known.[1] Permanent results in human economy demand accurate records of fatigue co-ordinated with records of achievement, and with records of the methods by which the achievement has been secured.

To find and apply the necessary measures for achievement and fatigue is primarily a task for the engineer. His training impresses him with the importance of measurement. His work makes him skilled in the use of measuring devices. Success in his profession depends chiefly upon the continued application of the most accurate measurement available, and this provides the incentive necessary for the maintenance of the scientific method. The engineer must secure the co-operation of the educator, the psychologist, the physiologist and the economist before he can hope to secure complete data, and to understand the full interpretation of what he finds,—but this is his duty

1. To make the investigation in the most scientific manner of which he is capable.
2. To submit his finds for comparative study by others and for the use of the world.

[1] See "Fatigue Study," Sturgis & Walton, 31 East 27th Street, New York.

This paper describes and attempts to make useful the history of such an investigation, a search for and the devising of satisfactory devices for measuring achievement.

It is a fortunate thing to be born in an age like the present, when the scientific spirit prevails in all fields, and where everything can be legitimately submitted to measurement. The world-wide desire to ascertain causes made it a simple matter to realise that large output or achievement was not in itself so important as the reasons for this achievement, with the consequent placing of the emphasis upon the methods *and* their results rather than upon the results alone. The writers thus became impressed early with the importance of obtaining as accurate and detailed records of methods as possible, if achievements were ever to be accurately measured.

This methods study was formulated into motion study, and divided into three parts:

1. Study of the variables of the worker.
2. Study of the variables of the surroundings, equipment and tools.
3. Study of the variables of the motion itself.[1]

[1] See "Motion Study," D. Van Nostrand, 25 Park Place, New York.

It was possible to make fairly satisfactory records of workers and of surroundings, equipment and tools with an ordinary camera. These were supplemented by descriptions in great detail of the best methods observed, even to the making of diagrams showing the relative location of the worker's feet and the position of the working equipment. Through such records conspicuous wastes in human energy became at once apparent, and various inventions of devices that cut down the amount of effort necessary, or eliminated needless fatigue, were made[1] With these inventions, and the comparison of the motions resulting from them with the motions used before the inventions, there was instantly an added appreciation of the importance of a study of the elements of the motions themselves.

With the writer's acquaintance with Dr. Taylor and his epoch-making discovery of the necessity for recording unit times, came an added appreciation of the need for including time study with motion study. The great problem was to record the motions used. The cinematograph was finally resorted to as an accurate recording

[1] See "Bricklaying System," Myron C. Clark, Chicago, Ill.

device. The invention of a special microchronometer that recorded times down to the millionth of an hour, made possible simultaneous records of this microchronometer and the positions of the worker whose activity was being studied. Even the first records, though unsatisfactory in many respects, demonstrated the practicability and usefulness of these methods of recording motions. Little by little the method was improved. An ordinary, reliable clock was placed alongside the microchronometer, in order to serve as a check upon its inaccuracy, if any occurred, and also to provide a record of the time of day that the study was made, in the resulting picture. Temperature and humidity records were included upon the picture. Signs, describing the place where the investigation was being made, the name of the investigator and the date, were placed for an instant in the field, and thus became a part of the permanent record. The original white dial with black marks was subsequently changed, at the suggestion of a film reader, to a black dial with white divisions and white hands that left a clear, sharp record upon the picture, and recorded the elapsed time of each exposure. The worker and the timepiece were placed in front of a cross-sectioned background, in order that the motions might be more accurately located. The ultimate value of these records, called "micromotion records," far exceeded what had originally been expected. These records were useful, not only in deriving improved methods of performing work that were worthy of being standardised, but also in serving as most admirable teaching devices.[1] The negative films were used originally for the study that resulted in the standards, and either these negative films, or positives that appeal more readily to those not trained in film observation, were thrown upon the screen, and served as topics for discussion in the foremen's, managers' and executives' meetings, or as demonstrations of the best methods of those learning the industry. Through the application of the results of data gathered from these films, large savings in industrial practices were immediately gained. As a typical example, where eighteen to twenty textile machines had been assembled in a certain shop before the application of micromotion study,

1 See "The Psychology of Management," Sturgis & Walton, 31 East 27th Street, New York.

sixty-six were assembled after the results of the study had been incorporated in the shop practice. The savings were the direct result of the micromotion study, combined with the improved placement or assignment of the workers to the work, and the improved surroundings, equipment and tools with which the work was done, that occurred in connection with it. We have here accurate devices for recording achievement and for measuring the amount of time consumed by the achievement. The motions that made up the method by which the achievement was secured are also here accurately recorded.

If the aim of making motion standards had been simply to provide instruction or time study data for those already skilled in the art of doing the work, the micromotion records would probably have answered every requirement, but, important as it is that those who know how to do the work in any fashion shall be taught the best way, it is even more important, for the savings, that the *learner shall be taught the best way immediately, that is, from the beginning of his practice.* When it came to the transference of skill, the micromotion records were not completely satisfactory in enabling the workers to visualise the path of the motion easily. The average engineer, who becomes, through his training and the necessities of his work, a good visualiser, even though he is not one by nature, often fails to realise the small capacity for visualisation possessed by the average person. A long experience in teaching in the industries made this fact impressive and led to the invention of the cyclegraph, and, later, the chronocyclegraph method of recording, in order to aid the non-visualising worker to grasp motion economy easily. The device for recording the path of the motion consisted of a small electric light attached to the forefinger or other moving part of the body of the worker. The worker performed the operation to be studied, and the path traversed by his hand was marked by a line of light. An ordinary photographic plate or film was exposed during the time that he performed the work, and recorded the motion path described by the light as a white line, something like a white wire. A stereoscopic camera enabled one to see this line in three dimensions. This line was called a "cyclegraph," since it had been determined a cycle was the most satisfactory unit of motions to be thus recorded, and the method was called the "cyclegraph method of motion study." A study of cyclegraphs shows a need for an indication of time, and, while the path of the motions is apparent, the *time* of the motions is not shown by the plain cyclegraph. This time element is of great importance, not only for securing records of comparative or *relative time,* but also for securing records of *exact time.* The time element was eventually obtained by placing an interrupter in the current, that transformed the white line of the cyclegraph into a series or line of dots and dashes. This made of the cyclegraph a chronocyclegraph. The exact time is secured by using a tuning fork vibrating a known number of times per second as an interrupter. The record now becomes a series of timed spots, and the method becomes the "chronocyclegraph method." Through intensive study of the apparatus, it has become possible to devise differentiated time and speed spots, and thus to distinguish various motion paths in the same stereograph (see Fig. 12). This means that we can now attach any desired number of lights to different working members of the worker's body, and

Fig. 11

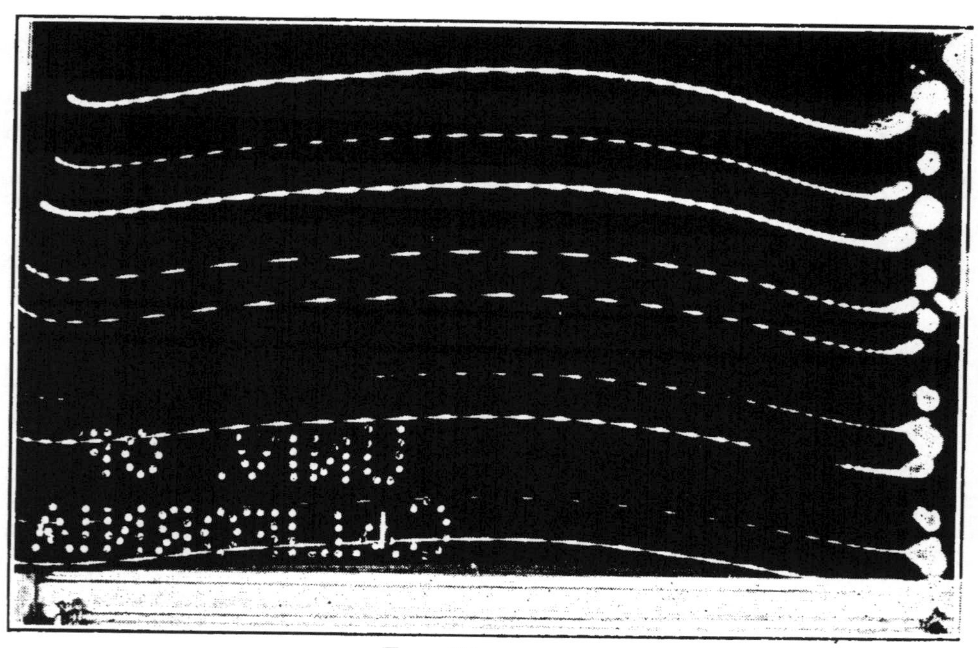

Fig. 12

Fig. 11

Types of cyclegraph apparatus for making the time spots in the paths of the motion.

Fig. 12

Types of lines of cyclegraph spots.

obtain synchronous chronocyclegraph records that are accurate, yet that differ in shape from one another to such an amount that it is possible to distinguish each, and to trace the continuous path of each light with ease.

The latest development in this study has been in the line of cheapening the cost of the apparatus. As in making micromotion studies it was found that the original method could be much cut down in cost by using the same film as many as sixteen times, so here it was found that cheaper types of interrupters can be used in place of the more adjustable tuning fork, made originally for the extremely accurate tests of the psychological laboratory. It must be understood that for the investigation of surgery and like types of activity, and for use in investigations in psychological laboratories, and in other scientific fields, the most expensive and elaborate of apparatus is none too fine; but it is possible, where first cost must be considered, and in much work in the industries, to make records accurate enough with apparatus that is within the reach of any one desiring to own it, and willing to devote time to learning to operate it.

With the study of the chronocyclegraph data has come the invention of the *penetrating screen,* which makes it easier to visualise and to measure the elements of the cycle being studied. It was desired to visualise simultaneously the time and space occupied by the motion. As is so often the case, invention was here held back by a belief. In this case it was, "Two objects cannot occupy the same space at the same time." It took years to realise that, while this is usually true, a photograph can show them as occupying the space at the same time. This multiple exposure method made it possible to place a cross-sectioned screen in any place, or number of places, in the picture. A screen may be placed in the plane in which the worker is performing his chief activity, before the worker, or back of him. The worker may be enclosed in a three, four, five, or six-sided box. The screen may be set at any angle. In short, a cross-sectioned screen of known dimensions can be introduced at any place where it will enable one to secure a more accurate record of the motion. This is done by the simplest and most inexpensive means. Take a sheet of black paper of the size of the space to be photographed, and

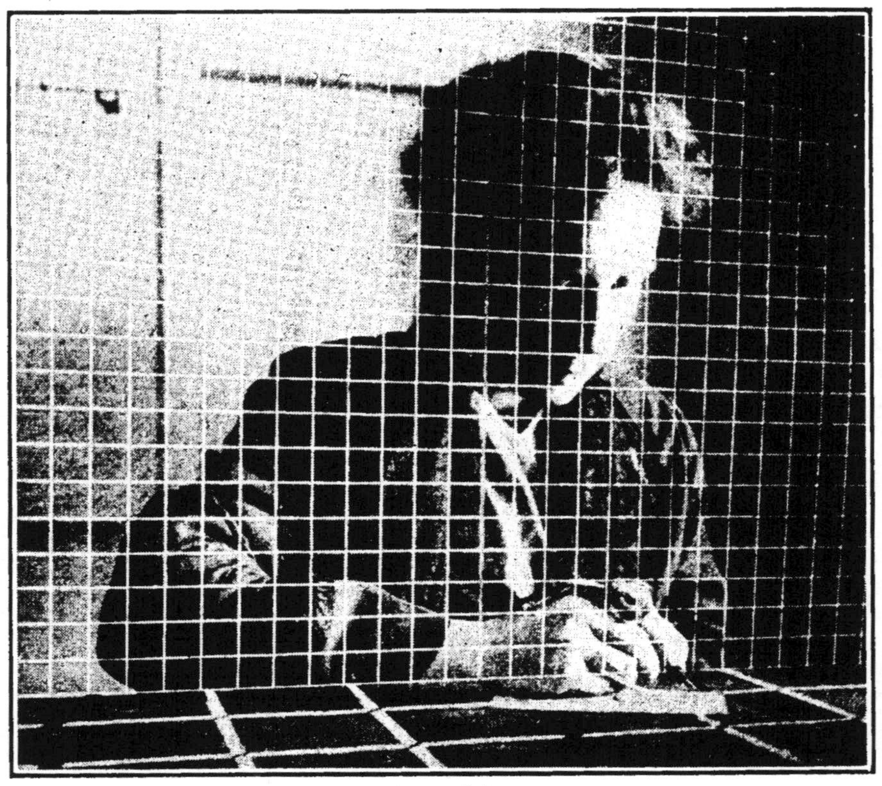

Fig. 13

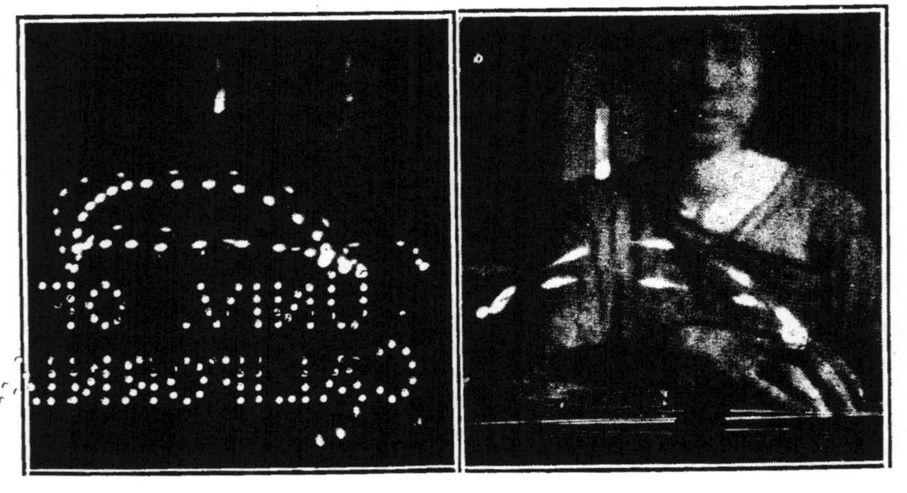

Fig. 14

Fig. 15

Fig. 13

First photograph of "penetrating screen" in the path of the motions. The screen is erected in the plane of the edge of the table and the hand, arm, and face are penetrated by it, as can be plainly seen in the stereoscopic record.

Fig. 14

First photograph of "Direction of Motion."

The pointed ends of the time spots show the direction of the motion.

Fig. 15

First photograph showing that fast motions and slow motions of the hands and arms do not occupy the same paths or orbits.

cross-section it with white lines at any distance that may be desired. Then photograph this screen at any place, or places, desired, by exposing the film each time that the screen is at a different pre-determined place. It is important that the time of the exposure of the screen be right, otherwise it may either be difficult to see the screen, or, on the other hand, the screen may be so prominent that it interferes with seeing the records of the motions themselves easily. The cross-sectioning being properly made, expose the now cross-sectioned film, and photograph upon it the work being studied. The resulting photograph gives the path of the motion laid along the cross-sectioned plane divided into any space elements desired. The penetrating screen, therefore, now furnishes the last desired feature for measuring and recording, namely, exact distance of motions. This, in combination with the foregoing list, now gives us records of exact speeds.

For some types of activity, such as handling a drill press, a record taken from one direction was satisfactory, and its close study enabled one to double the output of the machine with no added fatigue to the operator. With other operations, such as the folding of cloth, it was desirable to take chronocyclegraphs from several points simultaneously, in some cases placing the camera in front of the operator, at the right side, at the left side, and also above. A study of these records led to the realisation that it would be a great advantage, if it were possible to study the motion from all angles. An advantage to the motion study man in eliminating all useless, inefficient and ill-directed motions and in his general education in motion study. An advantage, also, to the worker, who could thus see his motions as he never could while doing the work. A special advantage to the learner desiring to acquire the skill in the shortest amount of time, and with the least amount of effort possible.

This need was even greater in the case of surgery, where it was found impossible, because of the necessity for operating conditions, to take the photographs required in the usual manner. While the telephoto lens was a great help in making it possible to take necessary records from the amphitheatre of the operating room, thus neither disturbing the operating conditions nor adding a new variable, through the presence of an observer, that might affect the methods used, here also the need for viewing the motion at other angles remained. An intensive study of this need and possible means for overcoming it resulted in the invention of the motion model. This consists of a wire model that exactly represents the path, speeds and directions of the motion studied. As many cyclegraph records of the operation taken from different angles as are needed are made, the cross-sectioned screen being introduced at those places where the direction of the motion makes a decided change. These cyclegraphs, which are in every case stereochronocyclegraphs, are studied through a stereoscope. Motion models are made by looking at the path as shown through the stereoscope, and bending the wire to conform to this path. The wire model, when completed, is placed in a black box cross-sectioned in white, the cross-sectioning being placed at the same relative places as are the cross-sectioned screens in the original picture. If the photograph taken from the same angle that the original photograph was taken is exactly similar to the original photograph, the model is considered a success. Each and every subdivision of a chronocyclegraph has its significance, and, therefore, the model must be brought to this state of perfection before it is considered complete. Where a chronocyclegraph motion model is desired, the spots on the chronocyclegraph are represented by spots painted upon the model. Black and grey paint being used upon the wire model that has been painted white, the result is spots of white fading through grey to black, that resemble closely in shape the white spots seen in the chronocyclegraph. It is possible also to use the ear in teaching. Through a new device consisting of a pendulum, a bell and a flashing lamp, time records, simultaneous with the other motion and time records, can be made. The same devices can be then set in operation while the work is being learned, and the learner can count by listening to the bell at the same time that he is learning through his eyes or his fingers by means of the motion model. The significance of all these devices to psychology and education can only be appreciated by a close examination of the models and cyclegraphs themselves, and an observation of their methods of recording *habit* or *lack of habit, decision* or *indecision, grace* or *awkwardness,* etc. Habit is best re-

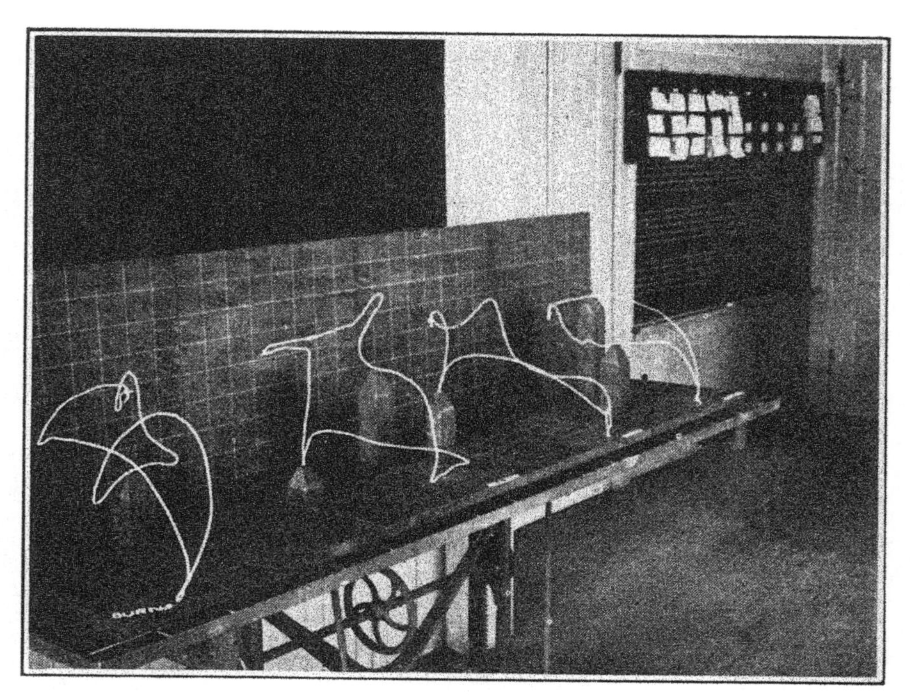

Fig. 16

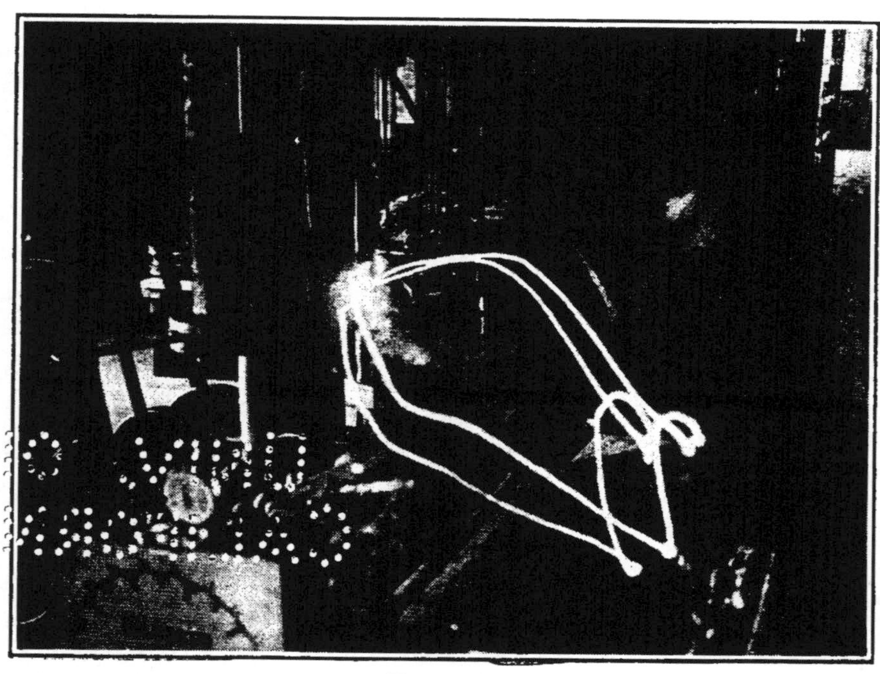

Fig. 17

FIG. 16

First photograph of wire models showing one man's progress of learning paths of least waste. These wires represent the paths of the left hand of a manager on a drill press,— a machine which he had not touched for twenty-five years.

FIG. 17

Chronocyclegraph showing two cycles of a foreman's left hand on the same machine,— showing habits of "positioning" before "transporting loaded."

corded by the stretched cyclegraph, which allows of the various lines recording habit being recorded accurately, yet in such a manner that they are easily distinguished from one another. These aspects of the motion models are important to the engineer in so far as he is a teacher and interested in the learning process.

Of perhaps greater importance, however, here, is the motion model as a means of devising, maintaining and improving standards. Through the study of the motion path, either as shown in the chronocyclegraph or in the chronocyclegraph motion model, and through a comparison of such graphs or models showing the paths of different operators doing the same kind of work, it is possible to deduce the most efficient method and to make this a standard. Moreover, each standard motion path is a help towards deducing other standard motion paths. Through an intensive study of motion paths followed in doing different kinds of work efficiently, there has come a recognition of the indications of an efficient motion, its smoothness, its lack of hesitation, its regular normal acceleration and retardation and its use of habit. The efficient method having been standardised, the motion model or cyclegraph then acts as a definite and tangible embodiment of this standard motion, thus enabling one to maintain the standard with comparative ease. It in no wise precludes improvement, nor suggests lack of progress toward the ideal. In fact, it suggests improvements because of its continued availability for observation and study. It furnishes a very definite starting point from which such improvements are to be made, as well as a measure by which they are to be rated and judged. Through a comparison of the motions used in different lines of work, in the industries, in surgery and in other kinds of activity, it can be shown that the same identical motions are used in doing what are usually considered widely different types of work. This allows of an instantaneous location of the place where skill is lacking, of a tremendous amount of transference of efficient methods from one trade, craft or profession to another; and of a consequent saving in time and energy. This is also the basis of our new classification of all activities in accordance with their motions and decisions. These models and graphs form also an important element in proper placement, since it is often possible to determine through them directly a worker's capability of learning and performing the work.

The data ascertained by these motion devices are placed upon the Simultaneous Motion Cycle chart. This analyses a motion cycle into its component parts, and indicates graphically by which member of the body, and in what method, each portion of the cycle is performed. The Simultaneous Motion Cycle chart is made on cross-sectioned paper with the various working members of the body used as column headings, and with the sixteen elements of the motion cycle placed vertically on the chart. By the comparison of the analysed motion model with the data on the chart, the possibility of the transference of work from one working member of the body to another is indicated, and the field for invention of devices or for more efficient placement is indicated. The Simultaneous Motion Cycle chart that is the outcome of the chronocyclegraph motion devices has been used by the writers for years in the industries, and has been presented by the writers for the benefit of the crippled soldiers, in whose interests they are at present engaged, with the collaboration of educators in Canada, England, France, Germany and Russia, in collecting data. The engineers of this country have been asked, through the American Society of Mechanical Engineers, to collect and send in all data available, that they may, by the use of this Simultaneous Motion Cycle chart and the models, be made available for teaching the most profitable motions to the crippled soldiers of all the warring countries abroad.

Important as the work for the crippled soldiers is, it is, as has been indicated, only a part of the conservation work that must be done. The other part, the conservation of all humanity to make good the great present loss, should be undertaken by a body like this Congress. No matter what work is done by the individual, or by individual plants, or trade groups, or industries, or even by a whole country, to cut down waste by standardising motions, there will be an enormous loss unless all nations co-operate in making and maintaining standards. There is no excuse here for holding secrets from one another, for reinventing, or for allowing any nation to fall behind the others. There is no excuse because the need is so overwhelming that all countries should hasten to start international standards. Let us use, therefore, chronocyclegraph motion devices as an aid towards making the much-needed international standards. This Pan-American Congress here assembled would serve as the most admirable headquarters for a Bureau of Pan-American Motion Standards. Undoubtedly, in every country here represented men have thought of the advisability of solving this great problem of human conservation, and have done what they could, each in his own restricted field, and largely without encouragement. It would be a wonderful help to these investigators, and to the world at large, if the work that has been gradually spreading from the individual to the group could now spread also from this representative group to the millions of individuals that it represents. The first step in this process is to enlist the interest of every member of this Congress in the necessity for human conservation, in the practicability of motion economy and in the belief that measured standards stimulate rather than stunt invention. The world must come to think of efficiency in terms of measured elements of motions and to concern itself with providing for efficient motions and sufficient rest for overcoming fatigue therefrom. This is not only a world problem and a pressing problem, but it is also a unifying problem. At war or at peace, every nation must realise the importance of the conservation of the human element. If we emphasise this, we not only make for efficiency in that more work may be accomplished with less effort, but we work also for permanent peace, in that we emphasise a common problem and suggest a common solution.

MOTION MODELS: THEIR USE IN THE TRANSFERENCE OF EXPERIENCE AND THE PRESENTATION OF COMPARATIVE RESULTS IN EDUCATIONAL METHODS [1]

This is the age of measurement. The motion model is a new device of measurement. It is for this reason that we are presenting the motion model to-day to this section of this Association, which stands for accurate measurement, and which believes that advancement must come through such measurement.

Your general subject for this meeting is listed as "The Scientific Study of Educational Problems." You are to be congratulated upon having chosen such a subject, and thus having shown your belief that advances in education, as in other fields of activity, depend upon the application of the scientific method to the solution of the vari-

1 Presented at a meeting of the American Association for the Advancement of Science.

ous problems involved. The *art* of teaching need never lose its ancient respect and standing, but the *science* of teaching, which in no wise supplants or interferes with the art, enlists a new co-operation from all those engaged in like types of activity, and should arouse a new interest in educators themselves. Only where the scientific method is applied can one expect to find invention that is improvement, and progress that is continuous and permanent.

Now the continuous application of the scientific method demands three things:

1. Units of measurement.
2. Methods of measurement.
3. Devices by which measurement can be made, and can be made at a decreasing cost.

Many such units, methods and devices of measurement, as applied to education, already exist. There has been in all fields where education is going on a lack of means by which behaviour could be accurately recorded, and the records used as data for predicting behaviour, and for outlining methods for attaining future desired results. *Motion models* supply this lack. They were derived in industrial experience, and were first applied in teaching in the industries, but their use is not limited to the industrial field, nor to teaching of manual operations.

The fact that this paper is presented here is indicative of the new feeling that is growing up in all fields of activity, of the necessity of correlation. This realisation of the importance of correlation is the outcome of many things. One is the tendency of this age to think in parts rather than in wholes, in elements rather than in grouped elements. In the olden times, both material things and human beings were invariably thought of as entities, wholes; but with closer thinking, and the awakening of the scientific spirit of analysis, measurement, standardisation and synthesis, has come the realisation that the fact that the thing or persons as a whole is often far less important than the fact that the thing or person is a group, or community, or combination of parts. The material thing is analysed into its elements. The human being is thought of as a group of working members. The old-time operation is thought of as a combination of acts. Now, finally, the motion itself is thought of as a cycle or combination of elements and motions.

With this intensive study of elements has come also a realisation of the importance of likenesses between things. This emphasis on likenesses may be given as the second reason for the realisation of the necessity of correlation. The old-time wise man wondered at the differences between things, and the scientist for years and decades followed the old-time wise man, and placed the emphasis in his classifications upon differences. Our ordinary classifications of to-day are thus based: for example, classifications of the trades are based more or less indefinitely upon

a. Difference between the types of men who do the work.
b. Differences in the ability and general education of the worker.
c. Differences in the kinds of, or the value of, materials handled.
d. Differences in the surrounding conditions.

Similar emphasis on difference marks the division of the trades from the professions, a difference so insisted upon that any attempt to correlate the work of, say, a surgeon, typist and bricklayer, meets with instant and almost universal disapproval. Yet the trend in science to-day makes it more and more apparent that all have neglected emphasising the likenesses to an astounding degree, and that a heavy price has been paid for this neglect. The very idea of difference implies division. This has set up for years boundaries between experiences, professional experiences and teaching experiences, that it will require yeoman work to destroy.

Yet splendid work is to-day being done in correlation. In the field of education the work done has not only a scientifically derived theory to support it, but can also show practical and successful results. This work is acting as a stimulus and a guide to workers in other fields of activity. Much undoubtedly remains to be done in correlating various types of teaching and learning in the schools, but what has been done is an indication of what can and will be done, and there need be no fear of the ultimate results. Educators are also to be congratulated on the beginnings made in correlating teaching in the schools and colleges and in the industries, such, for example, as in the half-time work now being increasingly introduced throughout the country. However, this correlation has usually been imperfect in that, while the teacher of such "half-time" pupils consciously adapts the school work to fit the shop needs of the pupils, the shop teacher and school teacher have not generally, as yet, compared methods and attempted to make the pupils' learning experience a unified one. Shop teaching, or to put it in a general phrase, "transference of skill and experience in the industries," is at present such an indefinite thing that one can scarcely blame either side for this lack of correlation. In this country, and in the same locality, are existing side by side to-day methods of teaching as old as the time of the guilds and the most modern methods of teaching, with an indefinite and surprisingly large number of steps, or grades of teaching, in between. It would undoubtedly interest, and it might profit, educators to trace the history of teaching in the industries; but this is not the place to present such a history. This, because the need for immediate correlation of teaching in the school and in the industry is so pressing and so great.

Never in the history of the world has there been such a need as there is to-day for economy in all lines, to compensate as far as possible for the enormous loss in human and material things caused by the great war. We have endeavoured to bring out in various recent papers the immensity of this loss, and to outline various methods by which it may be partially met. No body of thinkers realises more clearly than do the educators just what this loss means, and none have proved more ready to do their part toward meeting it, as is testified by the noble work done by educators in all the warring countries in standing ready and glad to do their part in the "making-good process."

We are presenting, therefore, what we believe to be the most advanced type of teaching in the industries, as a contribution towards that correlation for which we all long. This method is the result of years of experience as learners and teachers in many lines of activity. It has the increasing support of psychologists and teachers as well as of managers. We offer it not only hoping that it may prove of service in your various lines of activity, but with the assurance that you will immediately test it in every way possible by your own data and experience, and allow us to benefit by the results of the tests. We come with an equally hearty desire for co-operation, for this, in the final analysis, is the most satisfying incentive of all.

In order to make clear what this device, *the motion model,* is, and what the methods are in which it may be used, and by which it is used, it is necessary to trace, though only in outline, the history of its evolution.

The motion model is a wire representation of the path of a motion. It is the result of years of endeavour on our part to put a motion in such visible and tangible form that it may be visualised and measured with accuracy, and that the laws underlying

1. The behaviour that caused and affected the motion,
2. The behaviour that resulted from the motion,

may be scientifically determined. This desire to understand motions thoroughly has been a driving force with the writers ever since the start of motion study itself. The study of motions, of course, is not new. It must have existed, whether used consciously or not, ever since there was any activity at all; but what is now generally understood by the phrase "motion study" had its beginning in the year 1885. We quote here an earlier account, by one of the writers, of his first day at construction work. This will be of interest to this particular audience as not only outlining what occurred, but indicating to some extent the mental process that lay back of it. We quote:

"I started learning the work of the construction engineer on July 12, 1885, as I had been promised that a thorough mastering of at least one trade, and a general practical experience with many trades, would be followed by rapid promotion in my particular line of engineering. I was, accordingly, put to work between two specially selected, expert bricklayers, who were instructed that they were to teach me the trade as rapidly as possible. They gladly agreed to this. First one taught me, then the other, and, much to my surprise, they taught me entirely different methods. To make matters still more puzzling to me, I found that the methods that they taught me were not the methods that they themselves used. Now, I had the idea that, if I could learn one way thoroughly, I could be promoted in the shortest time possible to the higher position promised me. It seemed perfectly obvious that to learn two ways would take much longer than to learn one way, perhaps twice as long. Yet each man was an expert, whose methods were considered perfectly satisfactory, and each was turning out a large quantity of work excellent in quality. Hoping to discover which method taught me was the better, after a short time I quietly placed myself between two other bricklayers of my own selection. These were as willing to teach me as the first two had been, but I became more puzzled than ever when I found that their methods were different and that neither one taught me either of the methods shown me by my first two teachers. Naturally, the foreman soon sent me back from my own wanderings to my first location. All my friends, however, had one common rule for me, 'Keep at it on each brick until it is in true position.' I struggled on, trying to follow first one method and then another that was being taught me, and being constantly admonished by my first teacher, 'not to make so many motions.' Disgusted at my unsatisfactory results, I began watching this first teacher more closely, when he was working, and found that he used two entirely different sets of motions when doing his own work, both of these differing radically from the demonstration set that he used to teach me. That is, all three sets of motions were used to do identically the same type of work, the only difference being that Set One was used to teach the beginner, Set Two was used when working slowly, and Set Three was used when working rapidly. I looked at my second teacher. He also had three sets of motions. From that day I continued to observe as far and as fast as I could, and have found in practically every case that every worker has at least three distinct sets of motions for doing the same work.

"Naturally, as time went on, I came to ask my various teachers, 'What is the quickest way?' Each one had his own special 'kinks,' or short cuts, such as putting two bricks together in the air and then placing them together in the middle of the wall. Of course, I had to try out each of them, but soon found the great difficulty of achieving the first quality and, at the same time, using high speed motions while working.

"My observations involved certain fundamental questions:

"1. Why did the teacher use different motions when teaching than when himself working?

"2. Why did the teacher use different motions when working slowly than when working rapidly?

"3. Which of the three methods used was the right method?

"4. Why did each teacher observed have his own special set of short cuts, or 'kinks'?

"5. What was really the best method of doing the work?

"6. Was the insistence on quality first and right methods second advisable?

"7. At what speed should the beginner be taught to do his work?"

Through all these years we have been trying to find the reasons why the conditions that were so puzzling existed, and the answers to the questions here enumerated. Both reasons and answers depend upon a few simple and easily stated facts. We say "facts" advisedly, for the motion models have proved them to be such. We use the word with exultation, for, while we believed them to be facts for years, because the results justified the theories, we have often been ridiculed by students and investigators in all lines for so believing. Only since the motion models demonstrated the facts are they coming to be acknowledged as such, and are we receiving assistance in making them more generally useful.

The facts are as follows:

1. The motions are the elements to be considered in learning to perform an activity.

2. Right motions must be insisted upon from the beginner's first day at work.

3. Right motions do not lie in the consecutive acts of any one person performing the activity, unless he has been specially taught the standard method.

4. Fast motions are different from slow motions.

5. Standard speed of motions must be insisted upon from the learner's beginning on his first day, if least waste of learning is the first consideration.

6. Right motions at standard speed produce right quality.

7. The best learning process consists of producing right motions at the standard speed in accordance with the laws of habit formation.

We might here turn immediately to the motion model and show how it demonstrates these facts, but the demonstration will be clearer if the steps in the process of the derivation are carefully stated. We shall, therefore, return to the seven questions listed above, and state in each case our conclusions as to the answer.

1. The teacher used different motions when teaching than when working himself because he did not recognise his activity as consisting of motion elements. He attempted to demonstrate to the pupil that method that would obtain the desired quality of work product. He placed the emphasis on quality of output rather than on speed of learning.

2. The teacher used different motions when working slowly than when working rapidly because of the different muscle tension involved. When placing the emphasis upon speed, he was favourably affected by the variables of centri-

fugal force, inertia, momentum, combination of motions and play for position.[1] When there was no such emphasis on speed he was differently affected by these variables.

3. While none of the three methods of any individual worker was at all likely to be the standard method, the method used when working rapidly was most likely to approximate the standard.

4. Each teacher had his own short cuts in so far as he had consciously or unconsciously thought in motion economy. These differed because it was not customary to compare methods, because working conditions sometimes imply trade secrets, and because there was no adequate correlation between existing methods;— the eye being able to recognise the slow motions only.

5. The best method of doing the work did not at that time exist, because, due to lack of measuring methods and devices, it was not possible to record the elements, or motions, of all the different methods; to measure these, and to synthesize a standard method from the data.

[1] See "Motion Study," D. Van Nostrand Co., New York.

6. The insistence on quality first and right methods second was entirely wrong, since it allowed of the formation of wrong habits of motions, the result of which is a lifelong detriment to the user. The proper insistence is upon right methods at standard speed first, and quality of work product second. It must always be understood that absolute accuracy of method and speed occur simultaneously only with the desired quality. That is to say, take care of the method and the speed, and the quality will quickly take care of itself.

7. The beginner should be taught to do his work immediately with motions of standard speed. Quality should be attended to, however, in every instance.

a. By having the learner stop constructive work long enough to correct what he has done, or do it over again until it is of proper quality, care being taken not to confuse the doing with the correcting.

b. By having some one else correct the work as many times as is necessary, until it becomes of proper quality.

c. By having the learner work where the finest quality is not essential.

The determination as to which of these three methods for providing that the resulting product be of desired quality be used depends upon the type of work done and the type of learner.

It is probably needless to tell a gathering like this assembled here what a storm of adverse criticism the answers to these questions, embodying our beliefs, has caused in the engineering, and also in the educational world. In fact, this storm of criticism still rages to-day, and we expect many objections to the teaching process here involved from you at the close of this paper. We ask, however, at this point that you suspend judgment in this matter. Set aside all of your prejudices and even, perhaps, your experience, to put yourself into our attitude in working out what we have stated are the most efficient processes, and then at the conclusion strike the balance and assist us with your criticism.

You can see that all of our conclusions rest upon the possibility of examining and comparing motions and their results. The first necessity, then, was to obtain an accurate record of the motion. We used the fewest motions, shortest motions and least fatiguing motions possible. We wrote, and collected, descriptions of motions. We made diagrams of the surrounding conditions, even to the location of the worker's feet, at the time when efficient work was being done. We recorded the best we found by photography, at first with an ordinary camera,[1] later with stereoscopic cameras. These gave us detailed records in three dimensions. We used the cinematograph to record the motions being made against a cross-sectioned background, floor and workbench. This enabled us to record and follow the motions more accurately. We then invented a special microchronometer for placing in the picture, when we could find none in the market that could give us fine enough intervals to record the relative times of different motions. This micromotion process, with its combination of the cinematograph, the special timing devices and the cross-sectioned screen, enabled us to obtain accurate and satisfactory records of methods used, except

1 See "Bricklaying System," Myron C. Clark Company, Chicago, Ill.

that it did not enable us to visualise clearly the path taken by the motions and the elements of the motions.[1] Our next step was to attach a miniature electric light to the hand of the worker; to photograph the worker, while performing the operation being studied, and thus to obtain the motion path under actual working conditions. Through the use of an interrupter in the light circuit we obtained the photography of time in a single exposure. Later, through a time controlled interrupter, we obtained photographs of exact even periods of elapsed time of any desired duration. Through the use of a special arrangement we obtained time spots that were arrow-shaped that gave us the invention of the photography of direction. Through the use of the penetrating screen we obtained exact distance, and thus exact speed, of motions. Finally through the use of the chronocyclegraph method, which is a combination of these various devices, we obtained a satisfactory record of a motion path, showing relative time, exact time, relative speed, exact speed, and direction of all motions in three

1 See works of Muybridge, Marey, Amar.
See "Concrete System," Engineering News, New York.

dimensions. This chronocyclegraph now answers every requirement as a recording device, and also as a demonstrator of the correctness of our recommended practice, but it is not always a completely satisfactory device with which to demonstrate, simply because of the fact that the stereochronocyclegraph is not tangible. While it is possible to throw the stereoscopic records upon the screen, it is not satisfactory to enable an entire audience to visualise a motion path simultaneously. We were forced to use individual, single or magazine stereoscopes. As a result, any group of learners, although provided with stereoscopes and with the same picture, or cyclegraph record, find it difficult to use or visualise the cyclegraph simultaneously. It is difficult to concentrate the group mind upon the individual subdivisions of the motion. The motion models overcome this difficulty, making the motion path actually tangible. They enable us to demonstrate to the group mind.

The chronocyclegraph is a perfect record. It is free from the errors of prejudice, carelessness, and all other personal elements. The motion model is the precise record made tangible, and transformed into a satisfactory teaching device. We must, however, establish the validity of our records before enumerating the advantages of our teaching devices. What does the chronocyclegraph show? We group the following in accordance with the seven facts stated before:

1. The chronocyclegraph shows that the subdivision of the motion cycle is the important element. The motion cycle can be accurately recorded, hence analysed into elements that may be standardised and synthesized into a recorded method. The time taken to do the work cannot be used as a preliminary standard, the worker being allowed to use any set of motions that he desires. The elements of such a set not being scientifically determined, the user of the motions will either take longer than necessary to do the work, or become unnecessarily fatigued. In order to come within the time, he must finally arrive at what would at least be a habitual cycle of motions, many of which are inefficient. If any wrong habit of motions occurs there will be a serious loss later by reason of habit interference, with consequent unnecessary fatigue, and the likelihood of the time ever becoming standard will

be greatly reduced. The quality of the output cannot be made the preliminary standard, since this would allow of unstandardised motions, with an ensuing decrease of speed, and would result in unstandardised times.

2. The chronocyclegraph shows plainly the effects of habit. We have convincing illustrations of loss in efficiency due to the intrusion of old habits. They show that a discarded habit will return and obtrude itself when a new method is for some reason insisted upon, and the existing habit cycle is broken down in order that the new one may be formed. Say, the worker used originally habit A, and has come to use habit B. If he be taught cycle C, which differs from A and B, where he fails in C, he will be apt to introduce an element from A, not from B. The complication is evident. To profit by habit the laws of habit formation must be rigidly utilised.[1] These laws support the dictum, "Right motions first."

3. A comparison of the chronocyclegraphs of the various workers, studied in connection with

[1] See "The Psychology of Management," page 234, Sturgis & Walton Co., New York City.

the quantity and quality of the output achieved and with the standard method finally derived, shows that the best method does not lie in the motion cycle, or in the consecutive motion cycles, of any one individual. The micromotion records are of enormous benefit here, in that they enable us, at any time and place, to review the methods used by each worker, and to compare them.

4. The chronocyclegraph of the same worker performing the same work at different rates of speed demonstrated absolutely that fast motions are different from slow motions. They do not follow the same path or orbit. Micromotion records are here again of enormous assistance. Through them we were enabled to observe the worker performing the work at practically any speed that we may desire to see him use, as determined by the number of pictures projected per second on the screen. Those of you who have made a study of motion picture films, their making and projecting, and who have analysed trick films, where the people move far above, or below, the normal speed of real life, will at once realise the possibilities in motion analysis that lie here.

5. It having been shown that fast motions are different from slow motions, it becomes self-evident that, in accordance with the laws of habit formation, the learner must be taught the standard speed of motions from the first day. If he is not, he will not form properly the habit of using the forces that lie in his own body under his own control, of which he is usually at present unaware. It must not be understood that standard speed means always high speed. It does not. It means that rate of speed that will produce the desired results most efficiently. It must be remembered that there are a few motions that cannot be made at the standard speed at first by the beginner. In such cases the speed should be as near as possible that used by the expert.

6. The records of quantity and quality of output that are made simultaneously with the chronocyclegraph records demonstrate that right motions at the right speed produce the desired quality. This is, also, demonstrable through logic. The first thing to be standardised is the quality of the resulting product desired. The standard method is then made to be that method of performing the work that will produce this quality

most efficiently. Through performing the standard method at the correct speed the standard quality does and must invariably result. During the learning process, of course, quality will seem to go by the board, but this is only during the period that the learner cannot succeed in performing the method described. The correlation between the methods and the quality is perfect. Therefore, the expected and desired result must come to pass.

7. The teaching must, therefore, consist of two things:

a. The right method must be presented at the standard speed. The right method, taken with the cinematograph at standard speed of motions, may be presented slowly by projecting fewer pictures per second on the screen, but in any case the motions must be made at the standard speeds when being photographed.

b. The right method must be followed during the determining length of time, with the proper rest intervals for overcoming fatigue, and always with sufficient incentive.

The learning process is the proper repetition of the desired method at the standard speed.

It remains but to show the relation of the motion model to the chronocyclegraph, the use of the motion model for teaching, and for comparing the results of various methods of teaching. The motion models are made by observing the chronocyclegraph through the stereoscope, and bending a wire until it coincides with the path of the motion observed. The chronocyclegraph is best made in combination with the penetrating screen, that enables the motion model maker to measure, and thus to transfer to his wire very small elements of the motion path. The motion model maker is provided with a cross-sectioned background against which he can hold his model during the construction period, to compare his results with the cyclegraph from which he is working. He is also provided with a cross-sectioned box in which he may place the model, for observation and analysis. As the original cyclegraph, by means of the penetrating screen method, may be inclosed in a box of as many sides as are desired, it is often possible to facilitate the making of the model by the use of a properly cross-sectioned box. This box is of wood painted black, with the cross-sectioning done in white. The motion model, upon its completion, is painted black. The spots upon the chronocyclegraph are represented by spots painted upon the model. These spots are made of white paint, shading gradually through grey to black, and when finished resemble very closely in shape the pointed spots seen upon the chronocyclegraph. The motion model, which has now become a chronocyclegraph motion model, may be fastened against a cross-sectioned background and photographed from exactly the same viewpoint from which the chronocyclegraph was taken. The photograph of the model and the chronocyclegraph record may then be compared. Unless they are exactly similar the motion model is not considered a complete success. In cases where the motion cycle recorded is complicated, it is of great assistance to take chronocyclegraph records from several different viewpoints, as such records assist in making the motion model more perfect. In some cases two or more viewpoints can be obtained by mirrors.

The motion model has all the uses of the chronocyclegraph as a recorder of standards. In addition it has its teaching uses. The first of these is as assistance in visualising the motion path.

The motion model makes it possible actually to see the path that the motion traverses. It makes it possible to see this path from all angles. This was not possible with the chronocyclegraph, for, even where many chronocyclegraphs were made, the sum total of them only represented viewing the motion from the specific number of angles. The motion model can be viewed from all directions, from above, from below, and from all sides. A further importance of this in the industries is seen in the effect of the motion model upon the invention and redesigning of machinery to conform to least wasteful motions. The necessary limitations of shop conditions, machine operations, etc., make it often impossible to obtain a chronocyclegraph from more than one direction. Here we have all such limitations for viewing the motion removed. The motion model thus immediately educates its user by enabling him to see something that he has never before seen.

The motion model also teaches its user to make more intelligent use of chronocyclegraphs and cyclegraphs. These take on a new meaning when one has actually seen and used their corresponding models. In point of fact, a constant use of the motion model is a great help in visualising a motion path without a chronocyclegraph. Of course, such visualising cannot compare with the chronocyclegraph record, though it is often sufficient as a stimulus to motion economy and to invention. The motion model is also of use in that it enables one to teach the path of the motion. It makes it tangible. It makes the learner realise the problem of transportation involved. This has the byproduct of impressing the user with the value of motions. It is extremely difficult to demonstrate to the average person the reality and value, and especially the money value, of an intangible thing. The motion model makes this value apparent and impressive. It *makes tangible the fact that time is money, and that an unnecessary motion is money lost forever.*

The motion model is of peculiar value to its maker. The process of observing chronocyclegraphs and then bending the wire accordingly is not only excellent training in accurate observation, but impresses the maker, as probably nothing else could, with the importance of motions. He comes to be extremely interested in the significance of every curve and bend and twist and change of direction. ` He comes to realise the importance of the slightest change from a straight line, or a smooth curve. The elements in the motion cycle become apparent. He learns to think in elementary motions.

There are at least two methods, then, by which the models may be used to transfer experience.

1. By having the learner make such models.
2. By having the learner use such models.

The sequence with which these two methods should be used would be determined by the thing being taught, by the learner, by the teacher, and by many other variables. If the object of the teaching is to transfer some definite experience, or skill, in the shortest possible amount of time, it is better to give the completed model to the learner at the outset, and allow him to make a model later when he has learned the standard method, and may be stimulated to invention. If the object is to teach the learner the importance of motions and their elements, it is better to allow him to make a motion model first and to use the model later.

There is also a great difference between the method by which the motion model is used to teach the expert and to teach the beginner. The expert uses the motion model for learning the existing motion path and the possible lines for improvement. He notes the indications of an efficient motion, its smoothness, its grace, its strong marks of habit, its indication of decision and of lack of fatigue. Nothing but a close study of an efficient motion, as compared with the various stages of inefficiency through which it passed, can make clear these various indications. The changes from awkwardness to grace, from indecision or hesitation to decision, from imperfect habit to perfect habit, have a fascination to those interested which seems to increase constantly. The expert, then, takes the model in whatever stage it may be, and through its use charts the lines along which the progress towards a more efficient path can be obtained. The motion model is to the expert a "thought detonator," or a stimulus to invention. On the other hand, to the beginner who is a learner, the motion model is a completed thing, a standard, and it should be in the most perfect state possible before being given to him. Through its use he can see what he is to do, learn about it through his eye, follow the wire with his fingers, and thus accustom his muscles to the activity that they are expected to perform. Moreover, he can, through the speed indications, follow the path at the desired speed, by counting, or by the use of specially designed timing devices that appeal to his eye, to his ear, or to both simultaneously. All of the sense teaching is thus closely correlated. A further correlation through books or through oral instructions concerning the significance of what he sees and touches, makes the instruction highly efficient.

This method of instruction may seem at first applicable to manual work only, but, as with its use the importance of decisions and their relation to the motions becomes more apparent, it will be seen that the complete field of use has by no means as yet been completely charted. So much for the motion model as a means of transferring experience, or of teaching.

We next turn to the motion model as a means for recording results. We have already discussed at some length the motion model as a record of a method of performing an activity. It can also serve as a record of the individual's, that is, the learner's response to the teaching. If at various stages of the individual's learning process his behaviour be chronocyclegraphed and then motion modeled, and the results compared with the motion model, we have a very definite and visible standard of progress. If various individuals at the same stage of learning be thus handled, we have not only a record of their progress, but also a record of the value of the method being used. If proper test conditions be maintained, and other individuals be trained along a different method, and the various sets of motion models be then compared, we have a comparative record of results. It will be seen that this method of comparing results may be used even where the motion model has not in any way been used as a teacher. The results of any number of educational methods that manifest themselves in any form of behaviour may be compared.

We have also a method that will record fatigue, and that, therefore, will make possible the determination of rest periods, their length compared to working periods, and also their distribution throughout the hours of the day.[1]

We have said many times that there is no waste in the world to-day that equals the waste in needless, ineffective and ill-directed motions and their resulting unnecessary fatigue. This means that there are no savings that can be made to-day that can compare with those made by eliminating useless motions, and transforming ineffective and ill-directed motions into properly directed and efficient motions. "Motion Economy," "Savings" and "Waste Elimination" must be the watchwords of the day; savings not only in money, but in the mental and physical elements that produce the money and the durable satisfactions of life. It is for you to conserve, to utilise and to increase this intelligence by training all people, and especially the coming generation, to become *thinkers in elements of motions.* The greatest wealth of the nation consists of the intelligence and skill of its people.

[1] See "Fatigue Study," page 127, Sturgis & Walton Co., New York City.

MOTION STUDY FOR THE CRIPPLED SOLDIER [1]

To-day there are several million men living in Europe who have suffered the loss of limbs, faculties, or both, as a result of injuries in the great war. Before this war is over this number will be enormously increased. No one who has not actually seen hundreds of wounded soldiers writhing in agony in the cars or hospitals can fully realise the conditions that exist, but the pictures and accounts from the front have been so vivid that the whole world has been aroused to a concrete expression of sympathy and efforts to alleviate the immediate suffering.

However, there has been, as yet, little or no thought given to the permanent suffering that is by far the most serious aspect of the subject. What is to be done with these millions of cripples, when their injuries have been remedied as far as possible, and when they are obliged to become again a part of the working community?

[1] Presented at a meeting of the New York local section of The American Society of Mechanical Engineers.

At the close of the war the various countries now engaged in it will find themselves for years, and probably decades, fully occupied in devising ways and means for paying the interest on their enormous debts. They will not be able to pension adequately and properly to provide financially for their astounding numbers of incapacitated soldiers. Neither would any system of pensioning, if that were financially possible, completely solve the problem, since the large majority of such cripples will be helped more by being provided with interest and occupation than even by financial support. The great problem that faces the world to-day is, therefore, immediate and permanent provision for enabling these millions of crippled soldiers to become self-supporting. This is a world problem rather than a problem for those countries only that are directly involved in the war, and demands a world-wide solution.

The crippled soldiers are of many types, for this war is a war of all classes, and not of the professional soldiers only, as one is at times inclined to think. In all countries, men from the colleges, the professions, the shops and the factories are at the front along with the usual military force. The cripples, therefore, will be of all types, and vary in training and capability as well as in the injuries that they receive. We might, therefore, roughly classify them as follows:

a. Men who have done chiefly mental work.

b. Men who have done chiefly physical work, but whose capabilities will allow them to be transferred to mental work.

c. Men who have done physical work, and whose capabilities and inclinations are confined to physical work.

The first two classes can be handled with comparative ease when crippled. The third class presents the most difficult phase of the problem. This problem might be summarised as that of teaching and fitting cripples for some sort of productive work, and specially modifying and adapting the work to the individual capabilities, preferences, difficulties and shortcomings. The problem is an exaggerated new form of vocational guidance, vocational training, and systematic placement of men.

The educators have been quick to see their responsibilities in this work. They have provided, wherever possible, in existing or new institutions, opportunities for crippled brain workers to become productive, and have been ready and willing to devise opportunities and to furnish teaching for those previously engaged in physical work to learn and to use any mental work of which they are capable. They have, however, realised with equal rapidity their limitations in placing crippled soldiers whose bent is towards some type of physical work, as they have seen that this line of placement lies in the specialised field of the management engineer.

The engineer, both because of his training and practice, thinks largely in terms of physical capacity and its concrete results. The engineer of to-day emphasises the human element as a factor in accomplishing results, and it is his peculiar province to make this human element most efficient. Knowing that the authors had specialised for years in this type of work, educators in the various warring countries have urged them to attack this particular branch of the crippled soldiers' problem, and to put the results of modern management in general, and of motion study in particular, at the disposal of those in active charge of training the cripples. No great amount of urging was needed. The authors have, before and since the war began, crossed more than a dozen European frontiers, have visited many hospitals and recovery homes, and seen at first hand the frightful need, and return to this country not only with the desire to be of service, but with a definite plan as to how service can be most adequately rendered.

The method of attack of the problem is as follows: It is realised that the psychological feature is an important one. A prime necessity is to inspire the cripple with the feeling that he can remain, or become, a productive member of the community. This is done by gathering data as to cripples of various types who have succeeded in becoming useful and earning members of the community. These data consist of concrete examples of men, women, or children incapacitated in any way, who have been enabled by any possible means to be useful to themselves and to society. Such data have been and are being accumulated at an astonishing rate. They serve not only to encourage the cripple by suggesting that what has been done, can be done, but also by indicating immediate methods of attack upon individual problems. Back of all these individual illustrations, however, must lie a scientific method for attacking the general and the individual condition of each cripple, for diagnosing the particular case, and prescribing an adequate remedy. This is our contribution towards the solution of the problem.

The motion study method of attack considers the work to be done as a *demand* for certain motions, and the proposed worker as a *supply* of certain motions. It aims

a. To consider all work from the motion study standpoint,— to discover exactly,

1. What motions *have* been used for the work.
2. What motions *may* be used for the work.
3. What motions *must* be used for the work.

b. To discover what motions are possible to the proposed worker.

c. To determine which type of work may best be adapted to the worker, and how.

It may be well to state that motion study considers always three groups of variables, which, in the industries, are *a.* The variables of the worker.

b. The variables of the surroundings, equipment and tools.

c. The variables of the motions.

In adapting motion study to the crippled soldiers' problem, we are considering these same three groups.

We realise that our problem is twofold in its aspect. It consists of

a. Determining the type of work that the particular worker can best do.

b. Determining that method by which he can best be taught to do the work.

The teaching element is more important in this new phase of adequate placement than it has ever been before, because in every case a new or changed worker must be made useful, self-supporting and interested. That he become and remain interested implies the highest form of teaching and of learning.

The first step in adequate placement through motion study lies in visualising the motions used, or necessary, in any given type of work. The simultaneous motion cycle-chart is a device for recording and showing the interrelation of the individual motions and cycles of motions used in any method of performing any piece of work. This motion chart was devised and is used by us in our consulting work of motion study in the industries. Here we deal mostly with those who have the use of all their limbs and faculties, but the chart is equally applicable when dealing with cripples.

The elements of a cycle of decisions and motions, either running partly or wholly concurrently with other elements in the same or other cycles, consist of the following, arranged in varying sequences: 1. Search, 2. Find, 3. Select, 4. Grasp, 5. Position, 6. Assemble, 7. Use, 8. Disassemble, or take apart, 9. Inspect, 10. Transport, loaded, 11. Pre-position for next operation, 12. Release load, 13. Transport, empty, 14. Wait (unavoidable delay), 15. Wait (avoidable delay), 16. Rest (for overcoming fatigue).

The simultaneous motion cycle chart is best made on decimal cross-sectioned paper. The horizontal lines, reading from the top down, represent time. We have found that the thousandth of a minute is the best unit with which to work. The various vertical spaces are divided into ana-

SIMULTANEOUS CYCLE MOTION CHART

Assembling the Cross Bar Group

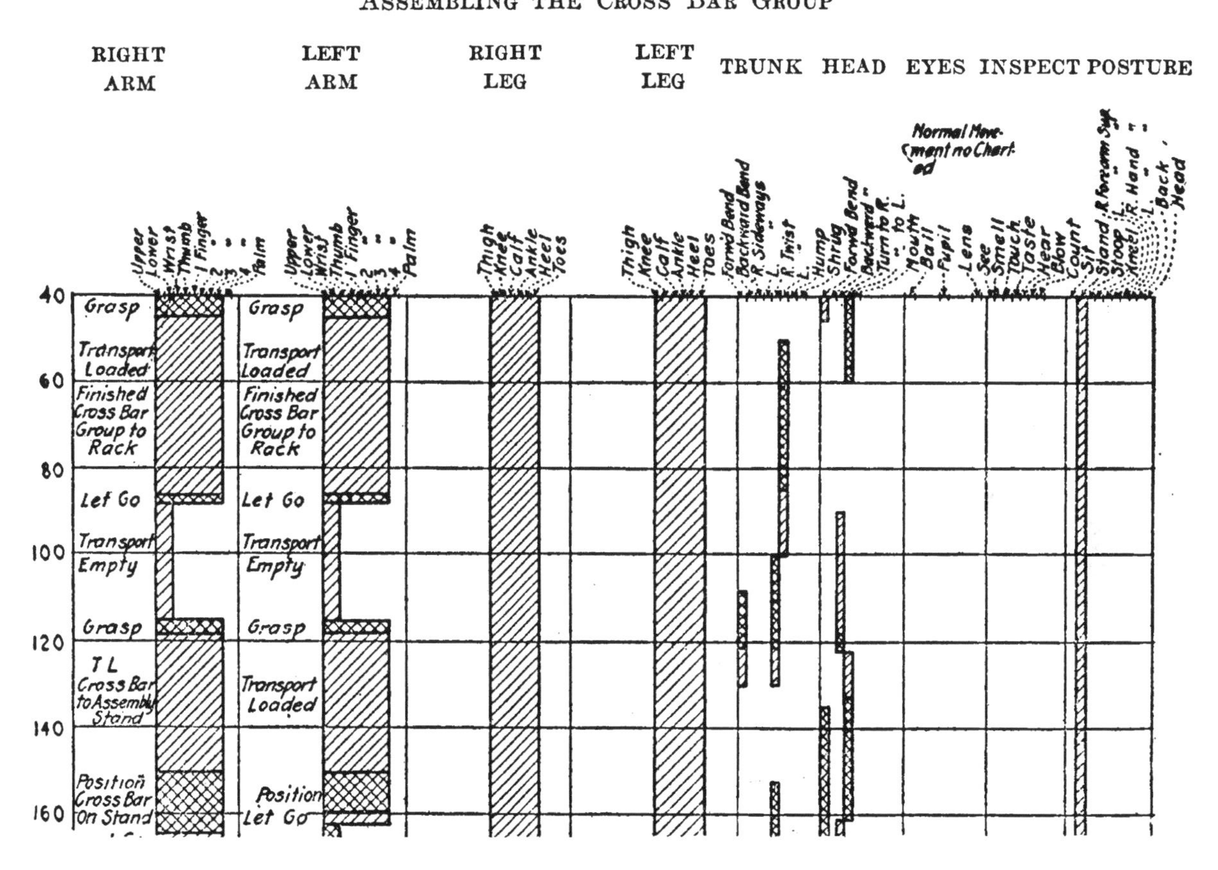

tomical groups, such as right arm and left arm, consisting of the subgroups, upper arm, lower arm, wrist, thumb, first finger, second finger, third, fourth, and palm; right leg and left leg, with the subgroups of thigh, knee, calf, ankle, heel and toes; trunk, with the subgroups of forward bend, backward bend, bend to right, bend to left, twist to right, twist to left, hump, and shrug; head, with the subgroups of forward bend, backward bend, turn to the right, turn to the left, and mouth; eyes, with the subgroups of ball, pupil and lens. There should also be the general heading of *inspection,* with the subdivisions of see, smell, touch, taste, hear, blow and count; and the heading *posture* with the subdivisions of sit, stand, kneel, stoop, right forearm supported, left forearm supported, right hand supported, left hand supported, back supported and head supported, etc.

Charting the data in this manner makes it possible at a glance to visualise a simultaneous cycle and the elements of the cycle of work done. The various motion cycles in the method under investigation are analysed into these elements. Through this analysis we are able to work out new sequences, cycles and methods of doing any type of work. Thus many types of work that have been formerly considered possible only for the man in complete possession of all his members and faculties can be adapted to the maimed or crippled worker. The chart shows in a concrete form which members and faculties of the associated units or working members of the human body are doing the work, are inefficiently occupied, or are available for doing parts or all of the work. They enable us to see at a glance not only how motions are at the present being made, but the possibilities of shifting these motions to other members of the worker's body. In other words, when using these charts for the crippled soldiers' work we are enabled to proceed immediately and directly to the more efficient rearrangement, distribution and assignment of the necessary motions to the different remaining members.

The data included in these charts are gathered through various methods of making motion studies, especially by the use of the micromotion method and the chronocyclegraph method of recording motion in the research laboratory. Here records of methods are made with special devices, microchronometer and the cinematograph, and also with the chronocyclegraph apparatus. The former type of records record the activity of the worker, the surroundings, equipment and tools, and also the time of the motions used. The latter records show the directions, speeds and paths of the motions. The records serve not only as data for the simultaneous motion cycle chart, but also as the most efficient of teaching devices. From the chronocyclegraph records are made motion models that not only make it possible for teacher and learner to visualise the desired motions from all viewpoints, but that also serve as path guides in case the worker taught is of the motor type.

Until recently, it has been considered good enough practice in the industries to teach the traditional or existing method of a successful workman. Through the methods and measuring devices of precision used in the motion study laboratory we are now able to record with exactness and in detail the methods of the most skilled workmen. By the use of the scientific method of analysis, measurement and synthesis we arrive at the method of least waste for performing the work. Through special teaching devices we then transfer the selected elements of skill and experience, in a new synthesised cycle of least waste, to workers who have never had that all around, non-guided experience or its slowly acquired skill. Not only are the methods transferred more efficiently but there is saving of time and effort to both teacher and learner, as is satisfactorily shown by learning curves of many past performances on widely varied types of work. The teaching devices, which we have specially adapted to appeal to as many types of workers as possible and to all available senses, are especially useful with crippled learners, where it is often necessary to specialise on some particular sense training.

The fatigue study that accompanies the motion study provides for the elimination of all unnecessary fatigue, and for adequate rest for overcoming necessary fatigue. Such study is imperative in the work with cripples, since the greatest of care must be taken that the maimed worker is not over-taxed.[1]

[1] See "Fatigue Study," Sturgis & Walton, New York.

While this method of attack brings gratifying results, no great headway can be made with the crippled soldiers' problem without worldwide co-operation. Such co-operation has been forthcoming wherever interest in the subject has been aroused. We gratefully acknowledge the receipt of suggestions and co-operation from members of our organisation, from friends in many parts of America and other countries, and particularly from the alumni and friends of our Summer School of Scientific Management, and we most earnestly beg for more and more. We need photographs, records and histories of cases where cripples have been made comfortable and less fatigued in their work, and have been taught and are successfully doing work in spite of their apparently insurmountable handicaps. The crippling is of every conceivable type, and every success will encourage some disheartened invalid to take up life with a new courage. We want also suggestions for adaptations of machines, tools, and other equipment or surroundings to workers. For example, we have found that typewriter manufacturers have made attachments for the use of operators having one hand only. We have seen such an operator handle the modified machine with satisfactory results. We have found that slight modification of other machines permits assigning their operating and controlling parts to the remaining limbs of the workers, and thus makes possible their successful handling by injured operators. Any kind of an adjustment or adaptation may be not only useful in its particular field, but may also form a missing link in an invention in an entirely different field. We will gladly take all data sent us and make them immediately useful to those working on the training of the injured soldiers in all countries. We have found it most efficient to think of all activity in terms of motions and decisions. Through more than thirty years of work in motion study we have facilities that make it possible to analyse all data into terms of motion economy, and thus to make them useful with the least waste in transmission or handling time.

This work of helping the crippled soldiers by teaching them to make the most of their motion possibilities should be the special contribution of the engineer in the field of social betterment. The opportunities for such work to-day are especially large because of the great war, but the methods that we now advise and use because of the great pressure will be available at all times. Through the reclamation service, if we may so call it, that we are using for the war cripples to-day, we are introducing a method that will never become unavailable or unnecessary.

We beg every member of the American Society of Mechanical Engineers to co-operate in this work, with us and with our friends abroad, who are waiting to pass on the data to those who need it so sorely. It is a work that is both timely and permanent. The need is sudden and new, but the data will be useful forever.

Discussion

Professor L. M. Wallace: It is indeed gratifying that such an able investigator as Mr. Gilbreth has consented to devote time and effort toward solving the problem of providing for the instruction of those disabled by the European war. That large numbers of young men of the highest type are being crippled for life is indeed as distressing as that so many are losing their lives in this great world calamity. It is my conviction that it is just as noble an undertaking to attempt to provide suitable means of preparing the disabled for useful vocations as it is to attempt to stop the terrible conflict or to provide means of first aid. Indeed, it is a greater thing than many realise, because it will mean untold benefit to thousands now deprived of those avenues of activity to which they have been accustomed. It will mean the fitting for useful vocations of thousands, who otherwise would be dependents upon society, which is always a greater burden to the one so afflicted than to those of society who bear the expense of such disability. I therefore hope Mr. Gilbreth and his associates may achieve much and that the members of this Society will rally to his support by extending encouragement, helpful suggestions and material assistance in the form of thought, labour, and money, if desired.

EDWARD VAN WINKLE: There is no question but what the adoption of a machine to a crippled soldier or a man without arms or legs is the duty of the mechanical engineer. I remember seeing the driver of a speed car, a man without arms, travel over a hundred miles an hour in a machine especially designed for him. The steering gear of the machine was adapted with shoulder yokes and the rest of the apparatus was operated by his feet. I saw him go from high speed forward to high speed backward inside of 50 ft., and he had a record of 108 miles an hour. There is no doubt that there are a number of instances of that kind in which with special machines cripples have been enabled to emulate those with full faculties.

W. Herman Greul inquired whether Mr. Gilbreth had outlined any standard method of reporting these instances which he could use in his tabulations. He wondered whether he had already tabulated the information which he desired, which would be very helpful in aiding the members to contribute.

Dr. Yeager, in his discussion, said, as a physician, he had been interested in cripples for a good many years, and in the course of his work he saw the necessity for providing means of occupation for many of these cripples. Some three years ago he opened a school for the training of men who had been maimed or injured or who, through some disease, were incapacitated from active work. In this school as patients were men sixteen up to thirty-five, who were taught reed work of all kinds, reed furniture making, rush seating and basket making. To the men who have the use of one and one-half hands, and whose minds are sufficiently developed, mechanical drawing is taught. For the men with one hand only, we selected glass mosaic work; a plan was devised for holding the glass so that with the one hand the worker could take his glass cutter, cut the piece of glass and fit it into the pattern he was making. We have taught show card writing, and also silversmithing.

As you will notice, most of these trades are for men who have the use of two good hands. Reed work needs two good hands. An encouraging feature of this work is that men who had never done any of this kind of work before, men who had never done any skilled work with their hands at all, would, in the very shortest space of time, become expert. I remember one young man, a structural iron worker, had an injury in which he lost one leg. He had no other trade, but he came to the school and became an expert silversmith; he did very beautiful work. He developed into a very fine draftsman, although he had no home training. He was a man from the very lowest circles, but the surroundings, the beautiful designs that we gave him, developed in him a desire for creating beautiful things, and he became a very skilled craftsman.

Another case was that of a young man who was born with his hands in an abnormal position, rendering them practically useless. We taught him show card writing. He held his pencil in his left hand, and he was able to draw and make letters very well. Another young man, whose right hand was paralysed, just had sufficient power to hold his paper and pen, to do mechanical drawing.

A man who had paralysis in both legs, and who needed two crutches, as both his legs dangled under him in a very unseemly fashion, learned the trade of chair caning, and during the summer vacation he managed to get the contract for a large club which needed several hundred chairs, and this cripple engaged ten able bodied men to work for him.

A boy with a very bad deformity of the hip needed two crutches to go about the workshop, but notwithstanding this he was able to work very well.

The work at this school is being done in the City of New York. It is the only school of its kind in the country, and whereas we have not attempted to get the men into work where machinery is required, we feel that we are filling a definite place in the work that we have done.

Mr. Hanau: When radium was discovered it was thought to be good for anything, for everything, for tuberculosis, for cancer, and for almost everything. The same remark applies to moving pictures. If you consider the moving picture, however, you must always keep in mind that it is a perspective. In the second place, you must keep in mind that the movements are not all in plane, so that they are very deceiving. To represent the three dimensions by photographs, you have to take them from the three sides, that is, the front, side and back projections. Then you can combine a movement which will be followed up very accurately. While this method is very good for efficiency, I do not think it is of very much value for just the purpose of this paper.

In working out data for members and other parts of the body for crippled soldiers, or maimed persons, one must be very careful. Such data cannot be represented only by a perspective picture, although perspective pictures are very valuable in shop practice.

F. Zur Nedden: A few weeks ago Mr. Gilbreth showed me a novel improvement of his method, giving the means for taking motion studies in the tri-dimensional way. For this purpose, Mr. Gilbreth first photographs a tri-dimensional net of white lights, he then removes the net, places the workman in position, and makes motion studies. By this way he can conceive, especially if he makes photographs stereoscopically, exactly the place every motion in space occurs. This would meet the objection raised by Mr. Hanau.

H. E. Resseler gave an instance of a mechanical device made recently in one of our hospitals in New York City. A young girl had a form of tetanus and by removing the muscles of the lower jawbone, and making a device with a spring, to be wound up just like one would wind up a clock, fastening it to the jaw and running it over the head, the jaw was kept in constant motion. After about three weeks the device was taken off. It was surprising to note how the muscles of the inferior maxillary had developed. The girl was then put to chewing gum, and the development of the muscles of the lower jawbone was continued.

JAMES GIBBONS: The work proposed to be carried out in Europe with a view to aiding crippled soldiers should hold a very important lesson for us in this country, because it seems it is an attempt to approach the efficiency question from another point of view than that which we are accustomed to. There is a tendency I think on the part of the efficiency engineer to pay more attention to the man of efficiency and to a certain extent discard the less efficient man, and a good deal of the opposition to efficiency methods which no doubt exists in the minds of many, and especially of workmen, is due to the feeling that the men naturally less efficient will be sacrificed to a great extent to those more efficient.

The fortunes of Europe are forcing upon men the necessity of taking care of their less efficient fellows.

From the point of view of the working public and from the point of the good of the country as a whole, this is perhaps the real foundation on which we should build on efficiency efforts — from the bottom up rather than from the top down; and I think we would be making a great mistake if with our own prosperity and our own good fortune in this country we should not give our careful attention to what is being done in Europe and watch carefully for the results which will come from this effort to raise the efficiency of those who are naturally inefficient.

W. N. POLAKOV: The paper by Mr. Gilbreth is of great importance, not only for the European problem of the near future, but for that in the United States, which is, so to speak, permanent, because industrial accidents happen and will happen in this country, although probably in diminishing proportion. It is well known to us how much money is being paid to the crippled soldiers of former wars, although if provision of some kind had been made in this country they could have been put to productive work and not be a burden on the country, but be productive members of society; but aside from that there was a question raised here whether it is in the domain of an engineer to look into this matter. In my opinion, it is most emphatically so, and I think we all owe Mr. Gilbreth thanks that he raised this question in our own Society.

The case of the crippled soldier is nothing but using the triple expansion human body as a compound, or something less than that, as it were, and therefore it is a problem of engineering, and of the works manager to adapt these conditions, or the men to the conditions, so that they will be useful. It is not so much the question of the selection of the man for the particular work, as the adaptation of the available man to the work which is to be done, whether the man is crippled or not.

As to the instruments devised by Mr. Gilbreth, I have watched and studied them in actual use, in the New England Butt Co.'s laboratory, although the details were too complicated to be explained in a short talk. The point of importance is that the motion shall be studied in order to save the waste motions and find out in what industrial processes certain limbs and certain parts of the body, certain muscles, are used.

In a factory where wearing apparel is sewn, the legs are absolutely unnecessary, as the machines are driven by a motor. In many other industries, when we consider it necessary to employ able-bodied men, we are doing a great injustice to those who are crippled, and more than that, we manifest our own lack of understanding. We do not want legs for the man who is working with his brains, and vice versa for the messenger boy it is not necessary for him to have two hands. For a telegraph operator two arms or two hands are entirely unnecessary, and many other examples could be cited.

Alvin Louis Schaller: I think that one of the points ought to be emphasised that Mr. Gilbreth brought out in his paper, and that is the psychic state in which the man must be brought before he can be made successful. The only reason why a cripple is so successful is because he has a will and a determination to devise his own methods for doing things.

I believe that one of the largest problems that Mr. Gilbreth had to confront when he began to reclaim these crippled soldiers was to get them into a state of mind where they could forget the discouragements into which they had probably fallen after receiving their wounds and realising that they would have to go through life in a crippled condition.

Robert Thurston Kent, who presented the paper, said: Last August I spent a day at Mr. Gilbreth's laboratory and saw what he had developed in the four years since I was associated with him, and Mr. Gilbreth converted me to a number of things that I believed were absolutely impossible two or three years ago, and I would suggest that all who are skeptical as to the value of the moving pictures of stereoscopic photographs and the three dimensions visit Mr. Gilbreth's laboratory, where they will learn a great deal.

The problem of efficiency or scientific management is to point out the job at which a man is a first-class man and put him in it.

Mr. Gilbreth has a standard method of tabulating. He lays out a chart divided into different groups, as explained in his paper — the head group, the different arm groups, etc., subdividing them into the forearm, the hand, thumb, and so on. By means of his photographs he finds out the relevant amount of time each member of the body is employed on a given job; he plots them on a vertical scale as to time. Striking a curve through these ordinates, he can see the relative importance of each particular member of the body in doing certain work.

The particular method employed is to take these charts and see if these motions of all the parts cannot be eliminated altogether, so that in the case of only a right hand motion, the motion of the left hand is gotten rid of, making it all a job on which the right hand only is employed.

THE PRACTICE OF SCIENTIFIC MANAGEMENT [1]

Scientific Management is simply management based upon measurement. Being thus based it must be not only the result of measurement, but also subject at every stage of its development to accurate measurement, and it must be willing to abide by the results of such measurement. The time has passed when Scientific Management can be content with basing its claim to being efficient upon the perfection of its theory. To-day such management must submit to accurate measurement of its practical results. It must demonstrate its value in practice.

In order to demonstrate this value of Scientific Management must show itself not only able to supply those needs of the employer and the employé that are supplied by any worth while system of management, but also its ability to supply needs that other types of management cannot supply, and its ability to meet and solve all problems raised by its peculiar and characteristic

[1] Presented at The Wisconsin Commercial and Industrial Congress, 1916.

methods. Any type of management that is worth rating as efficient

1. Must give to the employer a return on his investment and to the employé a fair living wage.
2. Must insure sanitary, healthful and standard working conditions.
3. Must insure a fair state of permanent co-operation between employer and employé. This would normally result from the maintenance of 1 and 2.

It is then the first duty of Scientific Management to establish, maintain and insure these fundamental working conditions. This it is bound to do, because in actual practice the maintenance of the entire system and the enjoyment of its advantages depend upon the employés being satisfied with their pay; working conditions being standard; and co-operation existing between all members of the organisation. For example, *A* is a worker in a plant under Scientific Management. It is usually not necessary for him to work harder than he would in a plant under traditional management, but he must work in accordance with specific instructions, and in order that he be willing to do this, and to fulfil the requirements exactly, it is necessary that he be paid more than the usual wage for that work in that vicinity. If he is not, in spite of the other advantages of working under Scientific Management, such as better teaching, more chance for advancement, a chance to specialise, etc., he is apt, because of the natural inertia of human nature, to choose to work in a plant where more "free and easy" and unstandardised conditions are the rule.

Working conditions in a scientifically managed plant must be standardised, and standard conditions must be the best possible, in order that the high output which makes possible the high pay may be made possible. *A* is working under foreman *B,* whose bonus depends upon the success in earning a bonus of the workers under him. His instructions and materials come from men whose bonuses are also connected with his bonus. Therefore, the condition of co-operation is maintained not only because of the *theoretic* necessity for such co-operation, but also because of the *practical* necessity for such co-operation, if all are to receive the high pay desired.

Besides providing constantly the three prime necessities for satisfactory relations between employer and employé, Scientific Management supplies to the employé five other benefits that, while connected with the three prime necessities, are not an essential part of them under ordinary management. The first of these is the opportunity for an increasing wage. While Scientific Management may be operated to some extent with day rate or with piece rate, it is customary, under practically all forms of such management, to introduce, at some stage in the development, some type of pay that allows of the worker's increasing his pay to the limit of his working capacity. The entire system is built upon the idea that it is to the advantage of every one that output be increased to the greatest extent possible. Increased output means increased wages. There are two questions that have been frequently asked just here. The first is, "Is increased output beneficial to every one?" The second is "Will the worker receive his fair share of the increased profit?" The first of these questions has been answered, as you well know, by the economists, and thinking people to-day have no doubt but that the world profits by any increase in output. The answer to the second question, that is, the decision as to the proper division of the profits from these outputs, is a question that must ultimately be answered by the economists also. Managers have answered it as best they could. Scientific Management answers by saying that the division must be such that the cost of the changes made by the new type of management are first deducted from the profits, and that these are then divided approximately equally between employer and employé. Naturally, the ideal division is such as will pay for the maintenance of the system, and satisfy both employer and employé. The division is usually, in practice, satisfactory, as is shown by the lack of strikes, and by the satisfaction of stockholders, as well as management and employés with the system itself. The average employé under Scientific Management receives a wage that increases

1. With his willingness to conform to instructions.
2. With his increased skill and intelligence.
3. With the resulting formation of efficient habits.

4. With his natural strength, ambition and endurance.

The second benefit that Scientific Management confers upon its users is regularity of employment. The manager realises early that it is too expensive a proposition to train a man to become an efficient member of the organisation, and then lose him because of lack of work, or poor arrangement of the dull and busy periods. Varions methods of providing regular employment are used. Typical of these are

1. Introducing a new type of work, for which equipment and workers are suited, that may be followed during the otherwise idle period.
2. Increasing, through advertising, salesmanship, etc., a demand for one staple product that will allow of specialising upon the production of that during light running time.
3. Teaching every employé various allied types of work, so that he may be shifted with ease to equalise the stress and to evenise exaggerated seasonal labour requirements of the working periods. This in no wise conflicts with the idea of functionalising the work and developing individuality in the workers,

but simply provides various outlets for the trained activity. The careful study of psychology makes it possible for us to teach workers who are to perform these allied activities, so that their habits in one line are a help rather than a hindrance in another. It is always best practice to insure that the lines of activity are similar in their demands for motion cycles, because of the enormous saving in habit formation.

4. Another method is by providing that in dull times highly paid specialised workers be retained even if necessary to have them placed on less remunerative, but more available work. For example, that foremen in a machine shop be put back on the machines. Such workers are paid what is in effect a retainer while on the lower priced work, which brings their earnings up to their usual amount. In this way the acquired skill and intelligence is kept in the organisation, and the outlay is reckoned as a good investment.

A third benefit of Scientific Management is the better placement of the employés. The ordinary type of management has no method of scientifically selecting the workers. The hiring is done by each foreman or perhaps rarely by a man or woman who has a "knack at it," "a fine sense of intuition," or "a deep knowledge of human nature." If the placement is successful, well and good. If not, the employé is summarily discharged and another selection made. Now, as has been already said, under Scientific Management there would be an enormous loss in a poor placement and in training an employé who is not fitted for the work. This supplies a very practical incentive to a careful examination of the applicant and a successful placement. It leads to the transformation of such jobs as that of messenger boy into training stations or observation stations, where a young applicant may be studied before his line of work is finally determined. It leads also to the utilisation of various tending jobs in the plant as such observation stations.

The fourth benefit is closely connected with the third. It is the opportunity for continuous advancement. All organisations of any type that can in any wise be rated as really efficient aim to hold their workers by offering a chance for definite advancement, but there is not usually a carefully determined path by which such advancement takes place. We have always believed that devising, using and maintaining a scientifically determined plan for promotion is a most important element in successful management. We have, therefore, made such a plan which we call "the three position plan," by which every member in the organisation is regarded constantly in relation to the three following positions,

a. The position that he last held in the organisation.
b. The position that he at present holds in the organisation.
c. The next position that he will hold.

In order that he may keep his present position, he must see that the position below, that he has previously held, is adequately filled, that is, he must be responsible for the teaching of his successor, and, moreover, in the advance to the next position he must learn the work done there thoroughly, that is, he must obtain adequate teaching from the holder of that position. Each worker is, then, constantly a learner as well as a teacher, and is a working member constantly of three groups. In one of these he is head man, in the other middle man, in the third end man. In practice this results in more rapid advancement, in more steady advancement, and in more rational advancement.

The fifth benefit has already been indicated in the fourth. This is the teaching supplied. To-day, when it is everywhere recognised that the problem of management is largely a problem of teaching, and that psychology is indispensable to efficient teaching, it is difficult to realise that less than four years ago this idea was greeted as radical, and that even to-day some of the foremost advocates of the best known type of Scientific Management consider that entirely too much emphasis is being laid on the psychological side. This audience, however, because of its peculiar training and experience, will be swift to recognise that the great solution of the employment problem and the management problem, like the solution of most social problems, lies in more education, and education is based on psychology, and gets its results from teaching. Because Scientific Management supplies teaching and provides that every member of the organisation be constantly both learner and teacher, it confers, perhaps, its greatest benefit upon those working under it.

The average student, investigator, or opponent of Scientific Management usually is willing, immediately or ultimately, to accept these claims, or better, demonstrations of Scientific Management as to its practical value. There are, however, two questions, or objections, according to the type of person making them, that are constantly raised against Scientific Management, and that are well worth the most serious consideration. The first is the question of fatigue, and the second is the question of monotony. The student asks

1. Does Scientific Management increase fatigue?
2. Does Scientific Management increase monotony?

The objector, or opponent, takes it for granted that "yes" answers both questions, and demands, "What are you going to do about increased fatigue?" and "What are you going to do about the soul killing, grinding monotony?" Since the milder queries of the student and investigator are implied in the strenuous demands of the opponents, it will, perhaps, be better to consider them in the latter more strenuous form.

What are we, who practice Scientific Management going to do about increased fatigue? We will state, first of all, that under Scientific Management fatigue is not increased. This for several reasons:

1. In many cases fatigue could not be increased, and the ordinary type of management is already resulting in the limit of fatigue.
2. Scientific Management believes undue and unnecessary fatigue is the worst form of waste.
3. Scientific Management knows that excess fatigue impairs the worker's capacity permanently.
4. Scientific Management, as a result of measurement alone, knows that the highest type of welfare, which implies no excess fatigue, alone makes adequate co-operation possible.

We maintain, then, that we are not increasing fatigue; on the other hand that, where excessive fatigue exists, we are cutting it down. Let us outline

1. What has been done.
2. What is being done.
3. What is to be done.

That is, let us review the past, view the present, and pre-view the future. We may, perhaps, be excused, since our aim at this time is to bring before you the practice of Scientific Management, for referring, in the remainder of this chapter, largely to our work, in that we can here with the greatest ease give you concrete examples of actual working practice. We realised early that fatigue is of two kinds,

1. Necessary fatigue.
2. Unnecessary fatigue.

that unnecessary fatigue is inexcusable, that only that amount of necessary fatigue must be permitted in a day from which the worker can recover during the interval from the close of one working day to the opening of the next. Naturally, the most efficiency, as well as the most humanitarian method is to eliminate all unnecessary fatigue possible, and to provide for such efficient rest periods that recovery from necessary fatigue may take place in the shortest amount of time, and with the greatest amount of satisfaction, possible.[1] We start, then, always, by making a fatigue survey of the particular plant or problem in hand, and determining, roughly if necessary, but as accurately as possible, what fatigue exists, and what proportion of it is necessary and what unnecessary. It is no easy thing to decide, what fatigue exists, or what fatigue is necessary, but one is safe to presume always that a large amount of fatigue does exist, and that an astounding proportion of it is unnecessary. There are some very simple signs of unnecessary fatigue; such as lack of chairs or rests of any kind, crowding, lack of light, lack of ventilation, lack of safety devices. The lacks themselves suggest the first facts in the necessities to be supplied. We have found the chair an admirable device upon which to specialise, since it is visible and tangible, and its supply, where it is lacking, usually goes a long way towards helping the organisation to think in terms of fatigue elimination. We adjust all work possible so that it may be done part of the time sitting and part of the time standing. We supply chairs, footrests and armrests; supply, or change, the posi-

[1] See "Fatigue Study," Sturgis & Walton, New York.

tion of the working equipment itself; use gravity; wherever possible consider effect of direction of motion on momentum and inertia; and, finally, make an intensive study of the motions being used, in order to derive and standardise more efficient and less fatiguing motions. We gather the existing devices into a little group called a museum, and add photographs of devices that might supply needs, taken from other places. We co-operate with the Posture League and the Safety First people, and other existing organisations that lessen the amount of pioneer work necessary to be done. We also attack the problem of work intervals and rest intervals, their length and their relation to one another. Along with this we start the Home Reading Box,[1] which is a method of putting literature of all kinds in the hands of all members of the organisation interested. This is a means of making the rest, or the recovery, periods more efficient. All of these things have been done, and are being done, and along with this we are to-day making intensive study of activity and its resulting fatigue. These studies are made by the

[1] See "Fatigue Study," Chap. IV.

chronocyclegraph method, and by making Simultaneons Motion Cycle Charts as a result of micromotion study. Work in this line has received a great impetus through the work being done for soldiers, crippled in all countries through the great war. With the peculiar type that will now come in enormous numbers into the industries, the fatigue problem becomes more than ever important. Where the old problem was to make it possible to do more work the new problem is, often, to make it possible to do any work at all. As for future work to be done upon fatigue, it will lie along the same lines as the past and present development.

It must be realised that fatigue is no problem that can be solved by hit or miss methods. Something, and a great deal better than nothing, can be done by any method of eliminating fatigue. Rest periods, no matter though they be not of the right length or scientifically distributed, are beneficial. Chairs, though not scientifically constructed, are far better than no chairs at all. We have received recently most helpful and constructive criticism from a professor interested in posture, who says that the average working chair has an unscientifically constructed back. We replied to him that, in most cases, we are so glad to get any chair at all, and so delighted when we have a chair whose height is prescribed by accurate measurement that we have been unwilling to dampen the enthusiasm of our co-operators by criticising the backs severely. Physiologists and psychologists must co-operate in the work of solving the fatigue problem. However, we feel that we have accurate methods of measurement to put at their disposal, and that the derivation of the necessary data for ideal fatigue eliminating and recovery providing devices must be a matter of time and careful application only. What does Scientific Management do about fatigue in practice? It eliminates all unnecessary fatigue that it can discover. It provides the rest intervals according to the best information available, and at the most scientifically determined intervals at hand. It also provides means for making these rest intervals efficient and profitable.

We turn now to the question of monotony. What do we mean by saying that work is monotonous? In the ordinary use of the term, undoubtedly, that it is tiresome, that it has sameness and great lack of variety, and that its result is a growing and a deadening fatigue. No one has realised more than those who devote their lives to the practice of the science of management that monotony is a very real and a very serious evil, that it exists in many kinds of work, and that it must be lessened or removed, if the work is to be truly profitable and satisfying. Now the natural and the right method of attacking the problem is to review first, the solution, or proposed solutions, of those who have previously considered it. There have been many of these. We might, perhaps, state five.

1. Insistence that there be no standard method of doing the work with a hope that the unstandardised conditions would render the work less tiresome.
2. "Leaving the initiative to the worker." This is simply another form of refusing to standardise the method, with the hope that the unstandardised conditions will spur the worker to invent a method for himself that will be of interest to him because he has been himself the inventor.
3. Shifting the worker from one type of work

to another, with the hope that the variety in the work done will rest the worker and will make the work interesting.

4. Moving the worker from one work place to another. This is a remedy applied usually by the worker himself, who leaves one plant or locality when he becomes tired of it and goes on to another in the hope of thus finding the longed for interest.

5. Welfare work of different kinds, which aims to supply the interest lacking in the work itself.

Now each of these proposed remedies is sure to prove futile, either immediately or in the long run, for the following reasons. The lack of a standard method is no insurance of variety, as the individual worker must, if he acquire any skill, gradually acquire also a standard method for doing the work, that is, a method, which is, at least, a standard for him. Leaving the initiative to the worker by no means insures that he will take the initiative. If he is not naturally of the inventive type, he is far more apt to copy the method of his next neighbour, which is as likely to be inefficient as efficient. Shifting from one kind of work to another, while it may for the time being interest a certain type of worker, is as likely to disgust another well marked type that has a decided hatred for changing work or working conditions. Moving from place to place, though usually indulged in only by those who crave excitement, is again likely to disgust those who dislike change, and welfare work, while excellent in itself and by far the best of these advocated remedies, has small, if any, preventive value.

The commendable feature of these attempts is, of course, the feeling that underlies them, that, if the worker is to accomplish the greatest amount of and the best work, monotony must be eliminated and the work made interesting. This feeling may be promoted by a humanitarian interest in the worker's welfare, or simply by a desire to get the most out of the worker. In any case, whatever this underlying cause, the results are to be commended.

The great difficulty and danger lies in the fact that the fundamental assumption at the base of all the remedies suggested is wrong. This assumption is, whether those who propose or use the remedies recognise it or not, that monotony and habit are in many ways related. There is a fundamental confusion between "monotonous" and "habitual." This confusion we all recognise when it is pointed out to us, yet it is strange that so few have ever noted this confusion that really lies at the base of the discussion, now reaching everywhere, as to the "monotony" of work, and its relation to the new types of management. We know, of course, that anything that is habitual is performed with comparative ease and dexterity. We know that habit simplifies. We know that it is the aim of all who desire to become efficient in any line to reduce as much as possible of the daily routine, in fact all of their activity, to habitual action. To the psychologist, habit has always been most important as a field of study, and little by little, all interested in industry have also come to appreciate the great force that lies in habit and its wonderful power for good or evil, as it is properly or improperly directed. We realise that habit cuts down fatigue, that it is easier to do anything that has become a habit, and that it tires one less. We realise that habit cuts out waste, that it allows us to accomplish more in less time, and thus gives us more free time to devote to other activities. Yet we seldom, either in conversation or in more careful thinking, fail to confuse habit and monotony. We do not for a moment believe that our every day acts of dressing and eating and walking are tiresome, or lack variety, because we do them the same way every time. Yet, when we come to the industries, and note habits of work there, and find industrial pioneers arguing for standardised habits, we immediately cry "Monotony," and the endless confusion begins.

Now, when we attempt to get down to the fundamentals of the matter we find that the habitual becomes monotonous only when there is no element of interest in what is being done, and when the higher mental powers that should be set free by habit, because they have nothing to do, go drearily over and over the mechanical acts that demand nothing of real attention. The monotony of housework, or farming, or different kinds of industrial work in the plant lies not in the fact that the work is habitual, but that it is uninteresting. The problem is not to break up habits, but to supply interests.

There can be no doubt, when one thinks the matter over carefully and logically, that the greatest good to all concerned can come only when every process possible is reduced to a habit. Methods must be standardised, that is, the best possible method must be found, prescribed, and become habitual with every worker doing the work. This is the first requirement. The second is that the element of interest be added to the work and be so incorporated that the work be never done without interest. This interest element may be added

1. By making the work itself interesting.
2. By making the results of the work interesting, so that the mind dwells on the results while the work is being done; that is to say, the interest may become part of the work either directly or indirectly.

The great means, in Scientific Management, by which work is standardised and interest added to t is motion study. The close relations between motion study and standardisation is based largely upon an appreciation by motion study of the importance of habit. Motion study starts always with an analysis of practice, and practice is only another name for existing habits of doing work. The first step is to make the record of the places, uses, and elements of existing habits. These are studied in the greatest detail. With the cause for every existing condition carefully determined, we take up the variables of the worker, the variables of the surroundings, equipment and tools, the variables of the motion itself, and in each case set down, in as great detail as is possible, exactly what the habit is, and to what stage of habit formation the activity has been carried in each case. From these very careful tests, and with the check of the most accurate timing possible, we determine the ideal habit for the particular work to be done. This is simply another name for standardising working conditions and methods, and the type of worker best suited for the work in hand. Having determined these ideal habits, the final step in reconstructing the process is to decide exactly how much may be made habit and exactly what must be left to decision. The process then becomes a series of decisions and motions. The motions cover the habit element. The decisions go a long way towards providing for the interest.

Let us suppose now that any type of work, formerly considered monotonous, is being done according to the methods prescribed by motion study, and let us see exactly how the element of monotony has been eliminated through motion study results. The method being used is as "habitual" as is possible, that is to say, the body is performing the same activity by as nearly as possible the same method every time, with the least possible amount of active attention on the work in hand. There is a careful allowance for fatigue. There is, therefore, no possibility of the body's becoming unduly tired. In the meantime, the active attention and all the higher power of the mind are free, free for the planning of details, free to plan new work, or free to do what they please. It would be much if motion study could claim only that it freed attention and these other higher powers to a much greater extent than did the older work methods, but the chief claim of motion study lies not in this freeing of the mind, but in the fact that it actually supplies work for the mind to do.

Just what, then, are these provisions for mental stimulus?

1. Motion study shows the worker a new method of attack. The study has been done with the worker's co-operation. He has, through the study, learned how a motion problem is attacked, and he can apply the same method of attack to the minutiæ of motions in his own work that the management has not had the time or the money to investigate.
2. The instruction card by which he works provides related items of interest that occupy his attention and stimulate to investigation.
3. The suggestion box that accompanies the installation of newer methods provides an incentive for invention that makes him want to devise better methods.
4. The new promotion plan, already mentioned, that accompanies motion study changes means that successful investigation will lead to advancement to the head of the function, to superintendence of some sort, or into the motion study or time study department.
5. The field of motion study and time study is in need of trained investigators in every in-

dustrial line, and this need may be filled by any skilled worker in any line of work.

6. Fatigue study, as already said, offers a great field of investigation. This field can never be investigated properly until skilled workers in every line of activity record individually and scientifically their own experience.

These are all direct elements of interest in the work itself.

As for the things that make the work indirectly interesting, such are

1. The home reading box, which stands ready with interest and amusement when working hours are over.
2. The high pay or shorter hours gained by the increase in output without extra fatigue, and all the outside interests that the high pay and short hours and the conserved strength and vitality make possible.

To sum up. Scientific Management, therefore, first shows that the problem of monotony is fundamentally different from its usual interpretation, and, second, solves the real problem of monotony by supplying that interest that is the natural eliminator of monotony. The close relationship between fatigue study and monotony study must have become apparent. Neither problem can be successfully solved without a simultaneous consideration and solution of the accompanying problem.

In conclusion, Scientific Management may not be ideal in theory nor perfect in practice, but all that it claims to be is management that not only is the result of measurement, but that is constantly willing to submit its results to measurement, because this is its basis. It is a part of the things that are real and lasting, and a knowledge of it and practice in it should be a part of the working equipment of every man or woman who wishes to take an active part in the world's work. It is doing much to-day that is not apparent. Its direct product, the comparatively few factories in which any so-called system is used and the comparatively few men who are earning their living through teaching the theory or installing the practice, are unimportant. The by-products are many and important. Men and women everywhere are realising that the remote *science* is really the near at hand *measurement;*

that life consists of motions and decisions; that satisfaction and interest, as well as efficiency, come from thinking in terms of elements of motions; that the great waste of the world lies in unnecessary fatigue; that "deadening monotony" is eliminated through interest.

THE THREE POSITION PLAN OF PROMOTION[1]

An adequate system of promotion is the solution not only of holding employés in an organisation, but also of the employment problem.

There is much emphasis to-day upon the proper *selection* of employés, and many and elaborate systems have been undertaken for a scientific, or near-scientific, *placement*. These are not in any wise to be criticised, for the selection of the individuals comprising any organisation is important, and any plan that will cause the employment manager to plan his duties carefully and to give each decision on the fortunes of others careful consideration is to be commended. It must be realised, however, that even more important is holding and helping these employés after they have been selected, and providing an adequate systematised plan of advancement for them. In

1 Reprinted from "The Annals" of the American Academy of Political and Social Science, Philadelphia, May, 1916. Publication No. 1001.

the Three Position Plan of Promotion we have not only the true and proved answer to the problem of promotion, but also the means by which efficient placement becomes almost automatic, and a supply of desirable applicants for any vacant position is constantly available. No system of placement can hope to succeed unless such a supply of applicants is available.

We wish to emphasise then three points:

1. The necessity of attracting desirable applicants.
2. The necessity of holding, fitting, and promoting those already employed.
3. The interdependence of these two.

We have never known a better friend of the worker than Mr. James Mapes Dodge, and he was wont to emphasise and demonstrate the benefit not only to the employé, but also to the organisation of holding the co-operating employé, and the great and needless loss to the organisation, to the worker, and to society in a constant change of the personnel of the organisation. Now, no organisation can hope to hold its members that does not consider not only the welfare of the organisation as a whole, but also the welfare of the individuals composing that organisation.

The Three Position Plan of Promotion considers each man as occupying three positions in the organisation, and considers these three positions as constantly changing in an upward spiral, as the man is promoted from the lowest position that he occupies and into the position next higher than the highest position that he occupies. The three positions are as follows: first, and lowest, the position that the man has last occupied in the organisation; second, the position that the man is occupying at present in the organisation; third, and highest, the position that the man will next occupy. In the third position the worker occupies the place of the teacher, this position being at the same time occupied by two other men, that is, by the worker doing the work, who receives little or no instruction in the duties of that position except in an emergency, and by the worker below who is learning the work. In the second position the worker is actually in charge of the work, and is constantly also the teacher of the man next below him, who will next occupy the position. He is also, in emergencies, a learner of the duties of his present position from the man above him. In the first position the worker occupies the place of learner, and is being constantly instructed by the man in the duties of the position immediately above.

Naturally a plan like this demands a close co-ordination of all positions. This is provided for through the master promotion chart. This chart is in the hands of the man in charge of promotion. It is slightly different for each organisation. It consists of a schematic arrangement of all positions in the organisation, so arranged as to provide for lines of most rapid advancement, along the various functions and subfunctions, under which the measured functional management by which we operate, works. The great advantage of such a chart is that it makes possible visualising the complete problem of the organisation's needs in teaching and preparing its members. The direct product of this is that the man in charge of promotion sees clearly the needs and the means of filling them, the demand and the supply. The important by-product is the gradual evolution of permanent, rapid, direct paths of promotion. This means the abolishment of the "blind alley" job, that is, a position into which some member of the organisation drifts with no chance for advancement. Another by-product of this chart is the fact that the promotion head, the promotion manager, or chief of promotion, as he has been variously called, can arrange for shifting or transferring the worker easily, if he sees that he has been improperly placed, or, if he develops abilities along some unexpected line. This is often the case under this type of management where there is great opportunity for the development of latent, as well as apparent, abilities. This master promotion chart is the great educative force to the management as to the importance of proper promotion.

The interests of the individual worker and his education as to the importance of promotion are carried on through the individual promotion charts. Upon these the records of each and every member of the organisation are separately kept. These sheets are often called "fortune sheets," and it is this aspect of them that is of peculiar interest to the psychologist. When a worker becomes an interested, or particularly co-operative or efficient member of the organisation he is called into the department in charge of advancement or promotion, and given one of these fortune sheets. Upon it is shown his present position, and he and the man in charge outline together his possible and probable line of advancement. The sheet then becomes his fortune map, or fortune schedule. The projected line of promotion is outlined in green, and upon it are placed the dates at which it is hoped he may reach the various stages of advancement. At set times the worker and the promotion chief, or one of his helpers, meet, and the line of actual progress of advancement of the worker is traced upon the map in red, with the dates of achieving the various positions. The two then consult as to existing conditions, the special reading and studying necessary for fitting for the new positions, possible changes, or betterments. The direct product of this is that the worker understands what he is doing, gets expert advice for greater progress, and realises that there is, and must be, co-operation between him and the promotion department for the good of all concerned. The by-products are equally, or more, important. One is that the worker is glad to impart all information that would be of help to the organisation as to his history and antecedents, his home and other social conditions outside the plant, that help or hinder his plans of preparing, ambitions, etc. It is common practice in these days to present the applicant with blanks to be filled in with all this information. We use such blanks in selecting applicants, always with the proviso that, if the applicant shows any disinclination to fill out such parts of the blank as tell of his ambitions or other details, which he may consider confidential, he be not required to do so. This information has been invariably volunteered, when the fortune map, or schedule, is understood. Naturally the applicant must furnish such information as will show his ability and reliability; but, as we will see later, these are so supplemented by data obtained through other sources that it is not necessary to ask for information usually considered confidential before it is volunteered. The second by-product of these fortune sheets is directly connected with the solution of the problem of getting constantly a group of desirable applicants from which to select more wisely. Thus, when the worker looks at his fortune sheet, and understands the three position plan of employment, he recognises that he must train some one to take his position before he can hope to be most rapidly advanced. Naturally he first looks around in the organisation to see who is available, for it is always desired that those within the organisation be advanced first. However, if no such person is available, he reviews his entire acquaintance, and all possible sources for new workers, in order that he may obtain the most desirable person easy to train into that position. It is not necessary to dwell long upon the advantages of this system for holding members already in the organisation. No worker who is constitutionally able to become a permanent member of an organisation will wish to change, if he is receiving adequate pay and has ample opportunity for advancement, especially, if, as here, he is a member of a group where it is to the advantage — more than that — actually to the selfish interest, of every member to push all higher members up, and to teach and fit others to advance from below. Inseparably associated with this is the fact that any worker will be ready and glad to enter an organisation where such conditions exist, and a desirable applicant will automatically present himself, when needed, at the direct request of some one who knows his particular fitness for the job, and desires him to have it. This selecting of the worker by the worker is real democracy. An organisation built thus has proved to be the most satisfying to both management and workers.

Now there are various questions that may arise concerning this subject, that it is well to answer here.

1. *What becomes of the workers who find exactly the positions that suit them, and have no desire to advance?*

The answer to this is that, if a worker finds such a position, he is retained in it, and that others who go beyond it are trained by him in the work of that position until they know enough about it to advance to the next higher grade. This often happens, especially in the case of the workers who prefer positions entailing comparatively little responsibility, and who, arriving at some work that satisfies them, and that involves but slight responsibility, choose to make that particular work a life vocation. If, as is seldom the case, a second worker is found who desires to remain in the same position, it is sometimes advisable to place such a contented specialist in another organisation, as trained and satisfied expert workers and teachers are all too rare.

2. *If promotion is constant, are not men constantly promoted or graduated out of the organisation?*

The answer to this is "Yes, and always to waiting and far better positions."

3. *What becomes of such well known "blind alley" jobs as that of elevator or errand boy?*

These positions are transformed into training stations or schools. Through them the young worker is put in touch with various lines of activity in the organisation and his possibilities, capabilities and tastes are noted. Tending jobs under this type of management are also so used as training stations. The new work for crippled soldiers, which is now occupying so much of our attention, is also furnishing a means of filling such "blind alley" jobs. A position that might be deadening for a young, ambitious boy, or for a progressive worker, might prove the salvation of a maimed, or crippled, worker who might otherwise become an idle, unproductive, and worst of all, a discouraged and unhappy member of the community.

4. *How can the close " human touch " that is essential to this system of promotion be maintained in a large organisation?*

We maintain this spirit through what we call the " Godfather Movement." This is especially successful where there are many young workers. Some older man in the organisation, preferably in the same department, or interested in the same line of work, is made the godfather of several young, or inexperienced, workers, and keeps in touch constantly with their progress. We call this man " the Godfather " in all foreign countries, where the relation between godparent and godchild is an unusually close one, and is very similar to the sort of relation supposed to exist here between members of the same family. It resembles, perhaps, in this country more the " Big Brother " or " Big Sister " Movement now so popular.

5. *What are the actual results of the workers*

already employed using this system of promotion?

They are most satisfactory in every case. In organisations where we have installed this system as a part of our plan of management we have seen

a. Office and messenger boys pass through five positions in one year.
b. A messenger boy become head storekeeper in three years.
c. A mechanic become night superintendent in four years.
d. A foreman become superintendent in two years.
e. A receiving clerk become head production clerk in three years.
f. A stenographer pass through five positions to motion study assistant in one year.
g. A stenographer pass through five positions to assistant chief of the three position plan in one and one-half years.
h. An office boy become assistant purchasing agent in three years.
i. A half time apprentice become foreman in three and one-half years.
j. A stenographer become head of the department of graphical presentation of statistics.
k. A labourer become superintendent in nine years.

and other cases too numerous to mention, many

advancing in spite of predicted dire failure of the plan of selection, placement and promotion. The greatest good is, perhaps, not the individual advancement, but the increased interest and zeal of all the workers under this plan.

6. *What are the practical results on supply of applicants and on better placement?*

In our experience we have never failed when using this plan of promotion to supply all needs of the organisation almost immediately with most desirable and efficient workers. Every member of the organisation working under this plan has become an active and successful "employment bureau man."

7. *What are the advantages of this whole plan to the man in charge of the function of employment?*

He benefits by this plan, perhaps, more than any one else. He comes in close touch with every member of the organisation. It is to the advantage of every member to tell him exactly which individuals he thinks had better follow him, whether these are inside or outside the organisation. Imagine for a moment that you are such a chief. *A* comes in and says, "Mr. Blank, I should like *O* to follow me in my position." *B* comes in and says, "I should like *O* to follow me in my position." *C* comes in and says, "Mr. Blank, I should like *O* to follow me in my position." Naturally you would recognise the wisdom of getting better acquainted with *O*. Or, perhaps, you suggest to *A*, "I think that *M* would be a good man to follow you," and *A* says, "No, I think I had better have some one else." You suggest *M* also to *B* and *C*, who reply somewhat along similar lines. There may be nothing fundamentally wrong with *M*, but the line you have planned will probably not receive as much co-operation as it should, and, in any case, there is something there worth investigating. Again, a worker comes to you and says, "Mr. Blank, I know a man who is not in this organisation who would be just the person to follow me. You know there is no one available just now, as the man below me is satisfied with his job." Here follow particulars as to the desired man's education, training, etc., which act as the supplementary data before mentioned. The recommender is given a blank form of "recommendation" to fill out for filing, whether or not the proposed man is hired. This naturally leads to the question

8. *Can any part of this plan of promotion be used without the other parts?*

The answer is "Yes" and "No." "No," if the desired results are to be obtained in full, since the entire system is interrelated and correlated with the complete plan of Measured Functional Management. "Yes," in that the fundamental ideas underlying this plan can undoubtedly be worked out in many ways. The immediate success of this plan is fostered by a carefully devised set of forms and charts and other devices for visualising the possibilities of individual success that have stood the test of time and use. The ultimate success of this plan depends upon the principles [1] that underly it, giving every man a square deal, a maximum chance for co-operation, advancement and prosperity, in other words, the opportunity for simultaneous individual and social development.

[1] See "The Psychology of Management," Sturgis & Walton, New York City.

THE EFFECT OF MOTION STUDY UPON THE WORKERS [1]

Motion study makes all activity interesting. While, at first thought, this fact may not seem of great importance, in reality it is the cause of many of the far-reaching results obtained through motion study. Motion study consists of analysing an activity into its smallest possible elements, and from the results synthesising a method of performing the activity that shall be more efficient,— the word "efficient" being used in its highest sense.

The process of motion study is such as to interest the worker. While undoubtedly some success could be made of motion study through a trained observer merely watching the worker, we find it of utmost importance and mutually advantageous from every standpoint, to gain the full and hearty co-operation of the worker at once,

[1] Reprinted from "The Annals" of the American Academy of Political and Social Science, Philadelphia, May, 1916. Publication No. 1000.

and to enlist him as a co-worker in the motion study from the moment the first investigation is made. Our methods of making motion study are by the use of the micromotion, simultaneous motion cycle chart, and chronocyclegraph methods. All make it imperative that the worker shall understand what is being done and why, and make it most profitable to every one that the worker shall be able, as well as willing, to help in the work of obtaining methods of least waste by means of motion study. While the process of making motion and time studies through the use of the cinematograph, the microchronometer and the cross-sectioned screen have been so reduced in cost as to make them indispensable even from the cost standpoint, the process is made even more economical when the worker, or the observed man, does his best work, and endeavours to take a part of active initiative in deriving the motion standards. We find in our practice that the worker is only too glad to do this. In fact, it is usually he, oftener than the observer, who cries out, "Wait a moment till this is done in the best way possible," or "Wait a moment, please, I know a way that I believe is easier." Similarly, when using the chronocyclegraph device; the worker is not only interested in the electric lights and their various paths and orbits of dots and dashes, but is most anxious that these paths shall be those of the greatest skill and the fewest number of motions possible.

The various methods used with these various types of apparatus, which are usually new to the worker, present problems in psychology which are interesting to the worker as well as to the observer. The worker is quick to note that, with the new conditions attending the measuring work, his own process varies for a short time at the beginning from his unusual habits, because of the entering of the variables of the apparatus and the strange conditions that it involves. He is quick to notice, also, that this effect of strangeness soon disappears, and that he then works exactly in accordance with his normal method. This period of strangeness, far from being a disadvantage, is, on the contrary, often a great advantage. The worker is almost *sure to revert to the former habit,* and an investigator or observer often gains valuable clues not only to excellent standards, but to necessary methods of teaching those standards, particularly with emphasis on eliminating interference of many wrong habits acquired in trade learning prior to conscious effort for motion economy. It is, therefore, clear that during the period of making motion studies the effect of them upon the worker is educative to the highest degree, for not only does he become interested in what he does, but he learns to think of all activity in terms of motions and elements of motions. The by-products of this are also important, as he is always able afterwards to learn new work much faster and with comparatively little coaching, and as he has that success that usually attends the work of one who knows the least wasteful method of attack of learning the new problems or performing the new task.

The effects of motion study are particularly striking upon the observer or the man actually making the studies. This is true not only during the time of making the observation, but also during the time spent in embodying the data derived in simultaneous cycle motion charts and in motion models. These motion models, which are wire representations of the paths of the motion, made from the stereoscopic records derived from the chronocyclegraph process have a peculiar educative value that is well embodied in the following statement of a young engineer who spent some time making motion models as a part of that thorough training for motion and time study man which we believe so necessary:

"After making a number of models of motions I have changed from a scoffer to a firm believer. I believe not only in their value as an aid to the study of the psychology of motions, but also as to their educational value in the teaching of the motion study man.

"I consider them of the same value to the motion study man as is the model of an engine or a mechanical device to an engineer. If the engineer was to study, for instance, a railroad engine, and the only chance he had to study was to watch an engine going by him at express train speed, his impression as to the mechanical working of the engine would be, to say the least, vague.

"A motion, in itself, is intangible, but a model of a motion gives one an altogether different viewpoint, as it seems to make one see more clearly that each motion leaves a definite path, which path may be subjected to analysis.

"I have made motion studies since making models, and what I learned from making the models has convinced me of their value. In former motion studies which I have made, my attention was always divided, more or less equally, between the direct distance between the starting and finishing points of the motion, the equipment, and the surroundings. I have found that, since seeing a motion, as represented by a model, I am better able to concentrate first on the motion itself, and then upon the variables which affect the motion. This seems to me a more logical method, and I know that I have had better results.

"I believe a good method of illustrating how a motion model helps one to visualise is to compare it with the wake left by an ocean liner. When one stands at the stern of a liner, which changes its course often, and watches the wake he can visualise the changes more readily than when unable to see the wake.".

It is interesting to note here not only the interest aroused intensively in the subject of motion study itself, but also extensively in the correlation of processes in the industries with general processes outside. The motion study man is a specialist who, because of his work, spends a large amount of time in the close study of motions, but to some extent this intensive and extensive interest is aroused in all those engaged in motion study, whether as observers or observed.

After the results of motion study are actually installed the effects are as great or greater upon those who work under the derived standards. It must be understood that *motion study* always implies *fatigue study*,[1] for the best and least wasteful results cannot be obtained otherwise, and that the worker who operates under these standards, therefore, not only has time to do the work in the best way, but ample time for adequate recovery from the fatigue of his work. This procedure provides directly for his physical and mental well-being. Motion study lays particular emphasis upon this. The great bogey of all who argue against standardisation is "the awful resulting monotony." Now psychology,[2] as well as the results in actual practice, proves that monotony comes not from performing the activity the same way every time, but from a *lack of interest involved in, or associated with, the activity.* This interest is supplied not only directly by motion study, but indirectly by the other parts of measured functional management, such as devices for eliminating unnecessary fatigue and for overcoming necessary fatigue.

Besides all this there is the interest aroused and the education resulting from the graphic representation of the results of motion study data to

1 See "Fatigue Study," Sturgis & Walton, New York City.

2 See "The Psychology of Management," Sturgis & Walton, New York City.

the worker as well as the observer. The pictures of the micromotion films are projected at the normal speed of the moving picture. They are also examined one at a time. The chronocyclegraphs in three dimensions are shown through the stereoscope, on the screen, by means of the wire motion models to the workers at the foremen's and workers' meetings and are there discussed. All the traditional knowledge is literally collected, measured, sorted, tagged and labelled. These data, together with indisputable measuring methods is presented before those possessing the greatest craft skill of the old methods, and who can quickest actually learn the new knowledge and put it to use. The new knowledge is of no use to the employer without the co-operation of the worker. This fact puts the relations between the worker and his employer on a new basis. They *must* co-operate, or both pay an awful price. These new methods have demonstrated that there is so much to learn that the employer cannot afford to put on and lay off his employés in proportion to the receipt of orders. He must solve the problem of steady employment. He cannot afford to let his specially trained men "get away." This is of vital importance in its effect upon the mental condition and activity of the worker.

By these means the workers, who are the actual producers of the nation, become familiar in every day experience with motion study and time study instruments of precision and with the results of their use. Such knowledge in the hands of our workers is the means of their being able to take the initiative in acquiring greater skill in all trades and in all life works. This is one of the best forms of industrial preparedness. It must be emphasised that the facts concerning motion study here stated embody not only a program but a record. The actual every day practice of motion study shows these effects upon the worker not only in the intangible results of added interest and a different attitude towards the work, but also in such tangible results as a larger number and a more profitable set of suggestions in the suggestion boxes, better attended and more profitable foremen's and workers' meetings, a greater number of promotions, more co-operation, more reading and study of the science of management, and higher wages earned with greater ease.

Motion study has no right to claim all the benefits that accrue from measured functional management, but, as a part of this management, it shares in these benefits, and thus those who work under it are assured of unusually high pay, during and after the motion study, a chance for promotion, physical and mental well-being, and a co-operative atmosphere in which to work. Motion study has the right to claim as its own benefits an added interest not only in the activity involved in the particular work done in the office or plant or wherever the work place may be, but in all activity away from as well as at work. Motion study benefits employés and employers, as well as everybody else who adopts its methods, because *it makes "to do," mean "to be interested," and to be interested means to be more efficient, more prosperous, and more happy.*

THE END

A FINAL NOTE

In writing this volume with the aim of eliminating waste, we realise that progress in general waste elimination is always retarded by the feeling that it is for others rather than ourselves. In order that we might practise what we preach, we requested that this book be printed in accordance with the forms of spelling recommended by the Simplified Spelling Board, New York City. The publishers ruled otherwise, and to change the spelling now would cause delay.

New conditions confront the world to-day. These new conditions demand as never before that savings be made whenever possible. Simpler Spelling requires less time to learn, saves motions of writing, typing, setting type and eye swing in reading. It saves ink, pencils, paper, and consequently helps save forests. The saving of forests in turn eliminates floods. The elimination of floods saves the priceless fertile soil from being eroded and washed to the seas, there to be lost forever.

Some of the greatest scholars in the English speaking world gathered together as the Simplified Spelling Board have made certain standards for simplification without any confusion or loss of any advantages of the present forms of spelling.

Simpler spelling has been adopted by over 300 schools, colleges and publishers during the last year. Its adoption is progressing faster than is generally realised. There is no logical argument against the forms recommended.

Ignorance and custom are the great hindrances to progress. Every possible saving in time, materials and fatigue that enables us to get more out of life should be adopted.

LILLIAN M. GILBRETH,
FRANK B. GILBRETH,
Member Advisory Council Simplified Spelling Board.

INDEX

Made in the USA
Columbia, SC
08 February 2020